To Za

Maggie

Hannah

With Best Wishes for

Great Success

[signature]

# "That's Not
a Fault…
It's a
Character Trait"

Also by Abraham J. Twerski, M.D.

*The Thin You Within You*
*Life's Too Short*
*When Do the Good Things Start?*
*Waking Up Just in Time*
*I'd Like to Call for Help, But I Don't Know the Number*
*I Didn't Ask to Be in This Family*
*Seek Sobriety, Find Serenity*

# "That's Not a Fault... It's a Character Trait"

*Abraham J. Twerski, M.D.*

St. Martin's Press ⚞ New York

Library of Congress Cataloging-in-Publication Data

Twerski, Abraham J.
  "That's not a fault . . . it's a character trait" /
by Abraham J. Twerski. — 1st St. Martin's ed.
     p.   cm.
   ISBN 0-312-19342-4 (hardcover)
   1.  Characters and characteristics.   I. Title.
 BF818.T94   1998
 155.2'3—dc21                   98-45098
                                     CIP

First St. Martin's Edition: January 1999

10  9  8  7  6  5  4  3  2  1

# Contents

# Introduction

Snoopy, Charlie Brown, Peppermint Patty, Linus, and all their friends, have become part of our lives. For decades millions of people have felt their day incomplete if they have not read the "Peanuts" comic strip. Sometimes we just smile at the antics of the Peanuts gang, but at other times it might occur to us that the strip has more than an entertainment quality. Something in that cartoon resonated for us.

And with good reason. The "Peanuts" characters are not really pure fiction. Rather, they represent many of our personality characteristics. Do we sometimes give up on something because we assume in advance that it is going to be a failure? Why, that sounds like Charlie Brown. Do we tend to cower before someone who tries to dominate us? That sounds like Linus frightened by Lucy.

The genius of Charles Schulz is that he has captured so many personality traits and demonstrated how they operate through his lovable characters. Gently he shows how some of these traits can have quite negative effects, and how we might benefit greatly if certain patterns were altered.

How do we know that there is a need for self-improvement? Is it realistic for every person to submit to an extensive psychological examination? I have a better idea for you. Let me show you what some of these character traits are, using the "Peanuts" gang as illustrations. This way, you may be able to begin your own psychological assessment.

The era of modern psychiatry and psychology is usually thought to have begun at the end of the nineteenth century, and, of course, the outstanding figure of that period was Sigmund Freud. In his many writings, Freud focused attention primarily on "neuroses." Generally speaking, a neurosis may be considered an emotional disorder occurring in an otherwise healthy personality, much like a cold or an infection that affects an otherwise healthy person. For decades, psychiatrists and psychologists were most interested in the treatment of neuroses.

However, the mental-health climate began to change, and around the 1940s, there began to be less emphasis in the psychiatric community on neuroses and increasing emphasis on "characterologic disorders." In contrast to an infection that affects an otherwise healthy person, a characterologic disorder is more analogous to a lifelong disease, such as diabetes. In the latter case, there is some physiologic problem that affects the entire system, rather than simply an isolated event. While diabetes is eminently treatable and those who have it may lead normal lives, it is clearly a different, more pervasive type of disorder than, say, a streptococcal ("strep") throat.

As a result of the change in focus in the psychiatric community, we began seeing more diagnoses, such as "passive-aggressive *personality*," "passive-dependent *personality*," "depressive *personality*," "narcissistic *personality*," etc. These diagnoses suggest something awry with the entire personality and are not singular anxiety attacks or hysterical paralyses.

Another difference between neuroses and character disorders is that the former are more easily recognized as abnormal phenomena, whereas character or personality disorders would seen to apply to many "normal" people. Some people are more assertive and aggressive, others are more passive. Some people have an optimistic perspective on life, while others seem to be looking at the world through dark glasses. There may not even be a line that distinguishes a clinical personality disorder from one of the variations of "normal"; it's often more of a blur.

Many people who would qualify for a diagnosis of personality disorder may go through life and function fairly well familially, socially, and occupationally. Many may even be successful in business or in the professions. These people may never see the inside of a psychiatrist's office. Yet the various personality disorders, even if considered "normal," may exact a heavy price. Although functional, these people may be quite unhappy, and may impose distress on others as well. They may not be able to fulfill their potential, which in turn may be another source of distress. It stands to reason that if a person were able to identify his or her own personality trait disorders and get rid of some negative features, life might be improved.

But this is easier said than done. If a person has a "neurotic" symptom—an obvious deviation from the normal—that causes him some inconvenience, he is likely to seek help to overcome it. A person may have a fear of heights that precludes her going to see her dentist, whose office is on the sixteenth floor, or a phobia of enclosed spaces, so she cannot enter an elevator. These symptoms may interfere sufficiently with daily life that the person feels the need to consult a psychiatrist or psychologist. This is not so true of the person who has a personality problem. Perhaps the person tends to be rather passive, but that is how he has been all his life. Maybe he fashioned himself after a parent who was passive, and this is just the way he is; what's "abnormal" about it?

A passive person may be working at the same level as several other people in a company, and may have adequate capacity for advancement. He may even be more resourceful than others. Yet when an opportunity occurs for advancement in the firm, it is the other person who gets it. Why? Because she is more assertive and does what is necessary to procure the advancement.

The passive person may then realize that he could have been elevated in the firm and gotten a higher salary. Although he did nothing to get it, he may resent the success of the other person, and this may cause a rift in their otherwise friendly relationship. Far worse, he may become angry with himself for not taking advantage of the opportunity. This anger can cause him to be grumpy. The frustration with himself and the depressed mood can result in his being irritable with his family. He may be "eating his heart out," which is an excellent colloquial description of the psychosomatic processes that may lead to heart disease, peptic ulcers, or compulsive overeating. Although this passivity may be thought to be "normal," it can give rise to much distress and dysfunction.

What should one do? Consult a psychiatrist or psychologist? This is quite unlikely when a person does not think of himself as being abnormal in any way. Indeed, he may see the advancement of his peer as being due to favoritism, and he may even begin to see his own lack of advancement as a sign of discrimination by his superiors. Furthermore, consulting a therapist requires a bit of assertiveness, which the passive person lacks.

But what if it were possible for a passive person to recognize his passivity as being self-defeating? What if he were able to see that while his behavior may not appear abnormal to anyone, it is nevertheless far from optimal? It is just possible that such recognition might motivate him sufficiently to do something to change, whether through therapy or self-help.

This is as true of other personality disorders as it is of passivity. People tend to not recognize that dysfunctional traits can be corrected, whether it be frank aggressivity, passive-aggressiveness, narcissism, or pessimism. They tend to accept these as unalterable givens, and resign themselves to what is in fact less than optimum function.

This is where Charles Schulz and his lovable characters come in. Traits exhibited by any one character do not necessarily exist with purity in "real life." That is, there may be a bit of Charlie Brown, a bit of Sally, and bit of Peppermint Patty all in one person. Recognition of any of these traits in ourselves may lead us to take a closer look at whether they may be causing us some dysfunction.

So join me in an entertaining, amusing, and educational adventure in observing—and learning from—the personalities of the "Peanuts" gang.

# Chapter 1

## Whose Fault Is It?

It appears that there are actually four rather than three essentials for life: food, shelter, clothing, and *someone to blame*. The ubiquity of blaming and the sometimes absurd rationalizations with which we hold others responsible for our own mistakes and misdeeds leaves no conclusion other than that blaming must serve some important function. The need to blame is a character trait. Notice how some people must blame routinely while others assume responsibility when something goes wrong.

How absurd can we get when we try to project our failures onto others?

Charlie Brown had arranged a date for Peppermint Patty, and introduced her to Pig-Pen. The two had a great deal of fun at the Valentine's Day dance, and Peppermint Patty felt that Pig-Pen was in love with her. This is what happens when Patty receives no further communication from Pig-Pen:

*Peanuts®* by Charles M. Schulz. Reprinted by permission of United Features Syndicate, Inc.

Peppermint Patty's statement is a classic one and could be a guiding principle for those whose character and psychology requires them to blame. It is always easy to find someone else to blame. All you have to do is be unreasonable.

Peppermint Patty continuously gets poor grades in school, simply because she does not attend to her school work. However, she finds it much easier to blame the teacher, again being totally unreasonable.

*Peanuts*® by Charles M. Schulz. Reprinted by permission of United Features Syndicate, Inc.

Rather than recognizing that it is her laziness that is responsible for her D-minuses, Patty wants to blame her teacher, accusing her of prejudice. For some people, blaming may provide a kind of temporary relief from emotional discomfort, as does alcohol and drugs for others. However, very much like alcohol or drugs, this relief is short-lived and is almost invariably followed by a worsening of the problem. Whereas awareness of having made a mistake could lead to rectifying one's behavior and thereby avoiding similar mistakes in the future, blaming allows one to avoid what one must do to correct things. Furthermore, blaming others only makes one angry at whoever one blames. And when anger is unjustified, it is always destructive.

Peppermint Patty is lazy. She stays up to all hours of the night watching television, and does not do her homework. She is not aware of what is going on in the classroom, and often falls asleep in class. Patty invariably gets D-minuses.

Patty could get good grades, but that would require studying, and studying means effort, an idea that does not excite Patty.

Peanuts® by Charles M. Schulz. Reprinted by permission of United Features Syndicate, Inc.

According to Patty's theory, she gets D-minuses because the teacher does not like her looks, which is certainly not Patty's fault. Since her appearance is not subject to change, she will continue to get poor grades whether or not she studies. Why, then, bother to exert herself when it is all going to be so futile? Patty's blaming is an excuse for not studying—and a rationalization for not being chosen a patrol person.

People who use blame to justify not doing things they don't like to do are by no means limited to blaming others. They may also seize upon any other excuse: It is quite common to have backaches that make it impossible for them to wash the walls, mow the lawn, or clean up the basement. I recall that as a child I capitalized on a doctor's hearing of a heart murmur, a totally innocent diagnosis I exploited to stay home from school because I was afraid of a bully. This, I admit, was an example of a character flaw which I hope at this stage in my life I have rectified.

Hypochondriasis is a commonly used avoidance tactic, because physical pain or disability legitimizes the lack of performance, not only for others but also for ourselves. A physical symptom allows us to think, "I really do want to do it, and in fact I will, as soon as the physical problem is resolved."

I recall, with more than a bit of guilt, the worry I caused my parents when I complained of shortness of breath. My parents were very indulging, and instead of being wise to my machinations, they took me to several heart specialists for evaluation, thereby causing me to begin believing my own lies. Family and friends who think they're being helpful to a hypochondriac by allowing for the excuses may actually reinforce avoidance tactics. Some, like Marcie below, get nipped on the hand for their trouble.

*Peanuts*® by Charles M. Schulz. Reprinted by permission of United Features Syndicate, Inc.

There is a tendency for psychiatrists and psychologists to treat a problem by trying to understand its roots. The theory is that if a person has insight into the "meaning" of a symptom, and can "work through" (whatever that means) the source of the problem, the symptom would disappear. This approach does not always work; all that happens with some psychiatric patients is

that they become quite enlightened, but do not feel any better—
and do not eliminate negative traits that are holding them back.

Some contemporary schools of parenting psychology would
tell Patty, "Turn off the television set and study, and *after that* we'll
try to figure out why you are so reluctant to study." They would
attack the symptom head on, leaving the explanations and the
blame for some later date. Patty would not like this, because she
does not want to make the effort to study. She would much rather
have some explanation now, and instead of studying, try to deal
with the underlying reason. That is far more acceptable to her.

*Peanuts®* by Charles M. Schulz. Reprinted by permission of United Features
Syndicate, Inc.

Now Patty can chew on this for a while instead of trying to
not fall asleep in class. Any explanation, logical or illogical, is acceptable as long as she is not compelled to do whatever she dis-
likes. I recall one young woman who repeatedly asked for tests to
evaluate the possibility that she had brain damage. She could not
achieve a passing grade she needed to get into college. She would

not accept any reassurances that her brain was fully intact. It became evident that she was actually hoping for a diagnosis of brain damage, because as devastating as that might be, she could use it as an excuse for whatever she wished to avoid. "You can't expect me to go to college. I can't learn. I'm brain damaged," or "You can't expect me to hold a job. I'm brain-damaged."

*Peanuts*® by Charles M. Schulz. Reprinted by permission of United Features Syndicate, Inc.

Patty concedes that her problem is that she does not study, but instead of seeing it as something correctable, she attributes this to a psychological deficit that she cannot overcome.

One of the classic methods of escaping unpleasant reality situations is simply to deny reality. Many people go through life denying the existence of realities they do not wish to accept. This is standard operating procedure for those who revise history to suit themselves. Since the past no longer confronts them, it is rather easy to rewrite history and tell others, as well as themselves, that things were really different than reality. To deny the reality of the present is a bit more tricky, yet when there is sufficient emotional distress in recognizing reality, we may deny the very things that stand right in front of our eyes.

*Peanuts®* by Charles M. Schulz. Reprinted by permission of United Features Syndicate, Inc.

Since Peppermint Patty has no intention of learning anything about Hannibal, she dismisses the problem by assuming that her homework assignment simply won't matter because school will be closed tomorrow. This is denial and is another aspect of blaming. It goes like this: Patty dismisses her work by assuming it will snow. When it doesn't she can literally blame the weather. How could she know the weatherman was going to be wrong? Therefore, her failure is not her fault.

Denial may take the form of blocking the awareness of a fact or, as with illusions, seeing something as different as it actually is. I have been told that some scientists who are heavily invested in a particular theory, for example, and conduct experiments to prove it, may actually distort the results of the experiment in favor of confirming their theory, while the facts actually disprove it.

*Peanuts®* by Charles M. Schulz. Reprinted by permission of United Features Syndicate, Inc.

Why do people fail? Sometimes it is for reasons beyond one's control, but quite often it is because people do not take responsibility for their actions, which makes the alterable problems grow worse. In Patty's case, her failure is the result of her laziness, a trait she could improve if she worked on it. Patty is by no means stupid. She simply does not want to apply the elbow grease needed for good grades. All the oil that is buried under the earth's crust cannot make engines run. Only when it is brought to the surface and processed can it be put to use.

Patty does not see things quite this way. She would prefer that the world reward her for her potential. Unfortunately for her, reality only rewards whatever potential is actually developed.

*Peanuts®* by Charles M. Schulz. Reprinted by permission of United Features Syndicate, Inc.

The world changes as science and technology advance, and reality requires adaptation to change. Humans are essentially creatures of habit, and it is much easier to continue doing what we have been accustomed to do. It is characteristic of people who drink excessively to reject treatment, asserting that it is because of their inconsiderate boss or nagging wife that they drink. The message is, "I don't have to change. Get my boss or wife to change and I'll be fine."

A while back, the police put a stop sign at the street corner near my home. Previously, motorists drove around that corner, perhaps with a minimum of deceleration. They continued doing so even after the conspicuous stop sign had been erected. I confess that I actually enjoyed watching the officers stop drivers who ignored the stop sign and continued to speed around the corner. And I bet two out of three motorists used the excuse that the stop sign was new to try to avoid a ticket.

*Peanuts®* by Charles M. Schulz. Reprinted by permission of United Features Syndicate, Inc.

The drivers were oblivious that reality had "switched channels," and tried blaming something else for their mistake.

Lawyers and accountants must keep current with changes in laws and regulations, and physicians must stay abreast of the latest medical advances. Similarly, parents should be aware of the current challenges confronting their children. Too often, parents try to raise their children the way they were raised, ignoring the fact that times have changed. We cannot blame society's change, the educational system, rap music, or anything else for our children's negative adaptations. Parents for whom the use of drugs was not an option in their early adolescence may not even consider the possibility that their twelve-year-old may be using marijuana, and such discovery comes as a terrible shock to them. Greater awareness of the changes might have helped them prepare for such challenges, resulting in either successful preventative efforts or more efficient handling of the problem when it was discovered.

Tradition certainly has its place, and the display of the portrait of the founder of a firm who established and operated the business for four decades, may convey a feeling of security and stability. But if the heirs continue to run the business in the age of computers as it was run in the days of the founders, they will soon find themselves in possession of an historic relic rather than a thriving business. And they will have to recognize that inability to flex is a negative character trait.

Reality does "switch channels," and if we fail to recognize this, we get D-minuses in life. A recovering alcoholic once said, "I had to accept the world for what it is rather than what I would like it to be." As children we may be permitted to live a life of fantasy. But if our parents are too indulgent and shield us from the harshness of reality, we may grow up to expect that things will always be the way we want them to be. When they are not, we will look for someone or something to blame.

If you observe babies, you will see that they put every object within reach into their mouth. To an infant, how something tastes is the measure of all reality. This normal behavior of infancy should be discarded as one matures. If we fail to help our babies make this adaptation, the mouth remains the primary appraiser of reality, which is one of the reasons why some people are compulsive overeaters. So who is to blame? The parents, the child as he matures, or the food that tastes "too good" to resist?

*Peanuts®* by Charles M. Schulz. Reprinted by permission of United Features
Syndicate, Inc.

People who fail at one thing may try to compensate by ex-
celling in something else. There is nothing wrong with this philosophy, if it is properly applied.

As a child, I was a rabid baseball fan. This was not a difficult
feat in the era of the all-time baseball greats, such as Babe Ruth,
Joe DiMaggio, Lou Gehrig, and "Double-No-Hit" Johnny Vander-
meer. I lived, ate, slept, and dreamt baseball. Nothing was more
precious to me than playing baseball. But alas! I could not hit the
ball to save my life, nor could I catch a ball. With these two short-
comings, I was never being picked for the team.

In a desperate effort to be allowed to play, I saved up enough
money to buy a coveted "Louisville Slugger" bat, and the kids on
the playground realized the bat and I were a "package deal"—either
I got to play or they didn't get to use the bat. After much haggling,
with each team captain insisting that the other side take me, I was
accepted on a team, with one condition: "We'll take him, but his
outs don't count."

This delusion that I was playing, though, didn't satisfy anyone. After several days of enduring through the meaningless ritual of striking out each time at bat, I surrendered the Louisville Slugger to the other kids and directed my efforts at studies, which resulted in superior work and midsemester advancement to a higher grade. The compensation of academic excellence for athletic failure worked in my interest. In this case, I did not blame, I adapted.

Poor Patty! She tried to do the reverse, but it just did not work well for her.

*Peanuts*® by Charles M. Schulz. Reprinted by permission of United Features Syndicate, Inc.

Patty's prowess in baseball might be somewhat soothing to her bruised ego, but it falls short of providing her with a real reward. Striking out Charlie Brown on three pitches did not compensate sufficiently for her D-minus performance in class. Of course this strip goes back to a time when baseball was primarily a male sport. Patty tries another route; she asks Mr. Brown to groom her for a skating match. Patty's preparation for the skating match unfortunately runs into a snag.

*Peanuts*® by Charles M. Schulz. Reprinted by permission of United Features Syndicate, Inc.

Again, Patty does not see this mishap as her fault. We can only guess what she told Mr. Brown while he was cutting her hair. Characteristically, she blames Charlie Brown for it.

We do love you, Patty. Of course, you are a bit extreme, but that is because you live in a cartoon strip as a caricature. We love you because you are part of each of us. We share your grief at the D-minuses, and we feel the chill of the unsympathetic world when we find that the shoulder we are leaning on is but a frigid snowman.

# Chapter 2

# Making Believe: Only Snoopy Can Excel in a Dream World

The beloved beagle Snoopy may well be thought of as the "flagship" of the Peanuts strip. For decades Snoopy has captured the hearts of young and old alike and shows no signs of waning popularity. Surely we must have found something very endearing about this dog that has given him a tenacious hold on us.

First, Snoopy is pure fantasy. Although dogs do have considerable mental activity, no one believes that a dog is capable of such highly sophisticated thought as Snoopy, and certainly no dog writes detective mysteries. For many of us, fantasy is a lifesaver because it is what makes harsh reality bearable. We buy a lottery ticket and fantasize having great wealth, free of the constant worry of paying overdue bills. We fantasize what we will do six months hence on vacation, a fantasy that allows us to escape from our feelings of insignificance and unworth, and dream of being acclaimed by an appreciative world. We fantasize when we sleep, and our daydreams are often as vivid as our nocturnal adventures. Life without fantasy would be unlivable, and a dog who dictates letters to a little yellow bird is the epitome of life-sustaining fantasy.

But Snoopy is more than just fantasy, because, you see, Snoopy fantasizes. In other words, we are fantasizing a dog that fantasizes. He pretends to be an ace pilot, chasing the notorious Red Baron, or a soldier behind enemy lines, or a lawyer trying difficult cases. A fantasy that fantasizes is something extra special, like fudge that is poured over a delicious scoop of ice cream.

But a person cannot live totally in a fantasy world. That would constitute a break with reality and this is the domain of the seriously mentally ill, who believe themselves to be God, or a prophet, or a world leader. More than that, any of us who replace fantasy or prefer fantasy all of the time, are going to collide with the real world. The inability to live realistically at the quotidian level is a negative character trait. A normal person must come back from fantasy to reality, which is what Snoopy does when he leaves his heroic escapades and realizes that he is, after all, totally dependent on Charlie Brown to bring him his supper. Snoopy takes us into his fantasy world and then brings us back to reality, and that is perhaps why we love him so.

Vacation trips are not necessarily fantasies, although we may fantasize about them for months in advance. They are somewhat analogous to fantasy, however, insofar as they are a kind of escape from reality. A father, for example, thoroughly annoyed by the buzzing and printouts of computers, the zooming up and down of high-speed elevators, the bumper-to-bumper traffic on the highways, and the stock market ribbon that parades across the screen, may wish to escape this technological drudgery and lead his brood back to nature, to the unspoiled wilds, the world of his childhood where he went fishing with his grandfather. But alas! These retreats are becoming increasingly scarce, and the camping grounds in the wild may be perilously close to the fast-food purveyors that spring up like mushrooms after a rain. The father's fantasy of leading his children back to the pristine Garden of Eden may be shattered by stark reality.

*Peanuts®* by Charles M. Schulz. Reprinted by permission of United Features
Syndicate, Inc.

This father may try to make the most of it and reminisce. He
may tell his children how he built campfires on the ground rather
than on the grates provided by the park service, and about rough-
ing it without piped-in water. As he turns on the battery operated
television, he may tell his children how it was in ancient times,
when he had to listen to the car radio to get the latest news. The
kids may be so impressed that they may ask whether there was
any danger of attack from Indian tribes.

*Peanuts®* by Charles M. Schulz. Reprinted by permission of United Features Syndicate, Inc.

The parent who easily flows in and out of fantasy will adapt, find the humor in the differences, and bring his family along for a different kind of adventure.

Some people fantasize small, some fantasize big, but fantasy is not limited to individuals. Nations may fantasize about the grandiosity of the past, and may contemplate world dominion. Small nations whose place on the map is hardly detectable may dream about taking over the world, even though there is not a shred of reality to support such a possibility.

*Peanuts®* by Charles M. Schulz. Reprinted by permission of United Features Syndicate, Inc.

A person's fantasy is by no means restricted to any particular theme. If we think a bit about our fantasies, we will discover their versatility.

Shall I share one of my fantasies with you? I daydream that I am conducting the Philharmonic Orchestra in Beethoven's Fifth Symphony. Indeed, when I hear one of the great musical master-pieces, I visualize myself conducting the orchestra, and when the music is not played according to my liking, I see myself having a tirade at the musicians, much as we are told the great conductors do during rehearsals. My first exposure to Beethoven's great sym-phony was a recording by the incomparable Arturo Toscanini, an interpretation that no one has ever equaled. Of course, since I cannot read a single note of a musical score, this is a fantasy that could never be realized—but it is a great escape.

How powerful such a fantasy can be is indicated by the fact that prior to my entering medical school, all applicants were re-quired to take a battery of psychological tests. I was later called in by the school psychologist who asked me, "Are you sure you want to be a doctor? Your tests show that you would want to be something like an orchestra conductor." I could only laugh about how my secret fantasies influenced my responses to the test questions, and how accurate the interpretation of the tests was!

It was uplifting for me to discover that I was not the only person to harbor such a fantasy. I watched a television program in which Danny Kaye, one of my favorite comedians and one of the most gifted humorists of all time, told about his secret fantasy of being an orchestra conductor. The only difference was that Danny Kaye had the means to actualize his fantasy, and did indeed conduct an orchestra, even though he could not read a musical score either. He also pointed out how treacherous a fantasy can be, because there is far more to conducting an orchestra than just waving a baton. He was so overwhelmed by the enormity of the task that he was almost unable to go through the motions.

This taught me much about fantasy. It may indeed be pleasant to fantasize, and the temporary escape from the rigors and tensions of reality may be quite harmless, as long as we do not get carried away by our own fantasy. Unfortunately, we may sometimes lose our way back from dreamland.

It has been said that "a neurotic is someone who builds castles in the sky, and a psychotic is someone who lives in them." If you come back down to earth, there is little harm in occasionally visiting the castles in the sky, but if you actually move into them, you are in deep trouble. For those of us with this plain old negative character trait like fantasizing too much, the difference is not so cut and dried.

We must have the ability to distinguish fantasy from reality. I have seen many marriages that begin with a fantasy of what life would be like with the man or women one loves. There are sometimes major incompatibilities between two people that are obscured by fantasy, and if the harshness of reality precludes the actualization of the fantasy, the relationship may deteriorate with grave consequences to both parties and to the children of that union. Unless each partner can step out of fantasy and adapt to reality, there will be trouble.

The genius of Schulz is in showing us both Snoopy's fantasies, and his return to reality.

*Peanuts®* by Charles M. Schulz. Reprinted by permission of United Features Syndicate, Inc.

Being an ace pilot can certainly be thrilling, but in this particular situation, acting out the fantasy would require remaining outdoors in the cold rain. Snoopy therefore abandons the fantasy, for the comfort and reality of a warm bed.

Snoopy has an ego. Although he is certainly loyal to Charlie Brown, he is essentially self-centered. He is concerned about gratifying his physical desires, and also tries to elevate his rather pathetic position of being just a dog, low man on the totem pole, through his fantasies. Sometimes when he's feeling particularly grandiose these themes come together, such as when he feels that the prime function of human beings should be to look after the welfare of dogs.

*Peanuts®* by Charles M. Schulz. Reprinted by permission of United Features Syndicate, Inc.

Snoopy has an abundance of fantasies. In one he is a world-famous attorney, and as such, he teaches us something about the legal profession.

*Peanuts®* by Charles M. Schulz. Reprinted by permission of United Features Syndicate, Inc.

Like Snoopy, we too may wonder whether the inscription etched in stone on the courthouse building is grounded in reality. We might wish that justice and truth would prevail everywhere, but the reality is somewhat different. Lawyers' responsibility is to look after the interests of their clients, and if true justice favors their adversary, they still must make every effort to win on their client's behalf, even if this is a distortion of justice.

*Peanuts*® by Charles M. Schulz. Reprinted by permission of United Features Syndicate, Inc.

An attorney may well be engaged to find an "egress" for his client, and that is what he must do. Does this imply that justice for all is a fantasy?

Grandiosity or feelings of superiority are expressions of one's spending too much time in a make-believe place. People have various ways of trying to show their superiority. One of the ways is to use highly technical terminology. As kids we used to talk Pig Latin to impress our friends that we had an esoteric language. Adults do the same thing: You may read a complicated medical report about a disease, or hear doctors discussing it, referring to it as "idiopathic." That is an impressive Latin term that means, "I don't know what in the world causes it." But heaven forbid that doctors should admit to the lay public that they are anything short of omniscient. Hence, "idiopathic" replaces "I don't know." This way a doctor can avoid getting down to the nitty gritty of Medicare and stay Olympian.

*Peanuts®* by Charles M. Schulz. Reprinted by permission of United Features Syndicate, Inc.

Lawyers are not much different. But let us not be critical of any more professions. After all, automobile mechanics are also experts at giving you mumbo jumbo about car parts that may not even exist. Words can be highly effective purveyors of fantasy, and we are likely to be taken by things that we cannot understand. That is why being grounded in the real world is so important.

Some people envision themselves as authors of best-selling books, with throngs of admirers queuing up for their autographs. The fantasy is great, might spin authors on, but if we live in a make-believe place we won't come down long enough to do the dirty work it takes to be a published writer. The road to authorship can be most frustrating, with a lopsided ratio of manuscript rejections to acceptances.

Let me again share a personal experience with you. My first attempt at writing a book was as a fledgling, first-year resident in psychiatry. My first critic was my dear wife, who tried to ease the blow a bit by saying, "It's really, good, honey, but it will be a lot better if you wait until you have had more experience working with people." This was my first rejection.

*Peanuts®* by Charles M. Schulz. Reprinted by permission of United Features Syndicate, Inc.

I then submitted my masterpiece to my teacher and mentor for his comment, and he returned it with a fatherly smile saying, "Put it away for a while, Abe. Not yet." I did as he said, and it was not until seventeen years later that I reread my manuscript, and was horrified at what I had written, thanking God that I had not been foolish enough to try and get it published.

*Peanuts*® by Charles M. Schulz. Reprinted by permission of United Features Syndicate, Inc.

I then took the theme I had begun with, the vital role of self-esteem in mental and emotional health, and rewrote it with much more maturity. This time I did submit it to a publisher, in fact to eighteen publishers, all of whom rejected it. This was beyond my comprehension. How was it possible that among eighteen different publishers, there was not a single one with good enough judgment to recognize a masterpiece of literature? (Here I was getting myself into make-believe, thinking I knew more than they.)

*Peanuts®* by Charles M. Schulz. Reprinted by permission of United Features Syndicate, Inc.

I then decided that while my thesis was certainly valid, the vehicle I had chosen was not palatable. I had essentially written a lecture, which was as tasteless and boring as most lectures are. The thing to do was to write fiction—a novel in which the characters would portray the various psychological hang-ups I was describing. In fact, I could even have some of the characters seeing a psychiatrist, and I would describe the proceedings of a psychotherapeutic session. I wrote two chapters of this adaptation, and when I read them, I had a violent episode of nausea. (Here, maybe, I was back with my feet on the ground!)

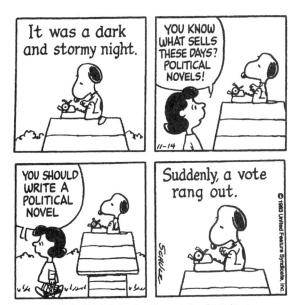

*Peanuts®* by Charles M. Schulz. Reprinted by permission of United Features Syndicate, Inc.

I abandoned the project for a year, and then rewrote it, neither as a didactic lecture nor as fiction, but by narrating vignettes, brief accounts of clinical cases where low self-esteem was at the root of the problem. I also made a few comments to stress the salient points that people might apply in their own lives. This final version, *Like Yourself and Others Will Too*, was accepted by a major publisher and enjoyed some measure of popularity for twelve years. Finally fantasy and reality had meshed.

One of the most intense drives people have is that of wielding power. In fact, the great psychologist, Alfred Adler, developed an entire theory of human behavior based on his belief that the drive for power was the dominant drive, at least among men.

We can see the lust for power in some people who clearly seek to be domineering, as those who seek high positions in government, whether by democratic means or by force. This urge must be overwhelming indeed. I cannot understand, for example, why a person who could live comfortably on his income would aspire to be President of the United States, with all the headaches and grief that come with that position, exposing oneself to the cruelty of vicious personal attacks and even an assassin's bullet. At least in modern times, the personal insults to the President are so great that they detract from the glory and honor of the position, and one can conclude only that it is the lust for power that is the motivating drive.

We are all vulnerable to the lure of power and not often in a positive way. The problem of spouse abuse, for example, which is so very prevalent, is primarily due to the desire to control, whether by emotional terror or brute force. Also, the person who drinks destructively and cannot accept the incontrovertible evidence that he is powerless over alcohol is being driven by the urge for power, which is sometimes blatantly expressed as "I can drink anyone under the table." The lust for power is also evident in adolescent gangs, and even in small children, who try to boss their juniors. And who does not remember playing "King of the Mountain" at age six?

What we lack in power in reality, we may possess in fantasy.

*Peanuts*® by Charles M. Schulz. Reprinted by permission of United Features Syndicate, Inc.

Some people like to boast about themselves and may spin tall tales about their great accomplishments, like the typical "fish" stories. This may come to a grinding halt when someone exposes them, and they may then feel quite foolish.

*Peanuts*® by Charles M. Schulz. Reprinted by permission of United Features Syndicate, Inc.

As we know, Snoopy has a complex about being only a dog. His fantasies lead him to think of himself as a snake, striking terror into the hearts of people. Fortunately for Snoopy, however, reality sets in, and he realizes that this would be "hard on the stomach." If only more of us had the good judgment that Snoopy has, we all might be happier people.

Snoopy is also a great lover, who can whisper endearing words of affection to capture the heart of his beloved. What young man has not dreamed of being so amorous that he enchants the fairest of all damsels? But here, too, reality asserts itself. What happens when these passions conflict with the growling of an empty stomach?

*Peanuts*® by Charles M. Schulz. Reprinted by permission of United Features
Syndicate, Inc.

One of the fundamental causes of a variety of people's problems is that they try to be what they are not. While some people think they are better than they really are, some people are afraid to show their true character but both live in fantasy worlds.

Let me backtrack a bit. As a rule, people are endowed with the necessary skills and resources to cope with reality. Sometimes people have a distorted self-concept and are not aware of their personality strengths, resulting in unwarranted feelings of inadequacy and inferiority. One possible reaction to this dissatisfaction with what one is or with what one believes he is, is to try and be something else.

The trouble is that while a person is well equipped to be what he *is,* he may not at all be well equipped to function as the new entity he *tries* to be, and his efforts in this direction are often fraught with failure.

*Peanuts*® by Charles M. Schulz. Reprinted by permission of United Features Syndicate, Inc.

Snoopy is a fine dog, and should have no difficulty living as a dog. But when he tries to be an alligator, he may suffer the unpleasant consequences of trying to be what he is not. That is as true for you and me, as it is for Snoopy.

The consequences of trying to be what one is not are not necessarily as destructive and painful as biting one's tongue. Sometimes they are more subtle.

"To thine own self be true." Very true words, because denying oneself and fantasizing oneself as being something else may result in severe psychological problems.

For example, I am not a perfectionist. I try to do things well, but I am not compulsive. Hence, when I thought I might become an accountant and I took courses in bookkeeping, I found that I was not suited for the job. Upon discovering a discrepancy of a few cents on the bottom of the ledger column, I could see no reason for laboriously researching all transactions entered into the books. It was so much easier just to add a few cents from my own pocket and proceed. Clearly, I did not have the perfectionism that is requisite for an accountant.

*Peanuts®* by Charles M. Schulz. Reprinted by permission of United Features Syndicate, Inc.

Luckily for me and Snoopy we are able to accept reality about ourselves and move on. Snoopy is too gentle to be a ferocious lion. Nor should one who cannot tolerate the sight of blood become a surgeon, regardless of how desirous that may seem.

Some people have a rather limited imagination, but others are prolific, like Snoopy, who is also a famous riverboat gambler. . . .

*Peanuts®* by Charles M. Schulz. Reprinted by permission of United Features Syndicate, Inc.

. . . and a commander of the Foreign Legion.

*Peanuts*® by Charles M. Schulz. Reprinted by permission of United Features Syndicate, Inc.

The genius of Schulz in presenting Snoopy as a fantasizer is evident in the way he interweaves Snoopy's many escapes into fantasy with his ultimate acceptance of reality. Some people get lost in their grandiose dreams and cannot make a satisfactory adjustment to factual reality. Their frustration at not being able to live out their fantasy world robs them of peace of mind.

*Peanuts*® by Charles M. Schulz. Reprinted by permission of United Features Syndicate, Inc.

Snoopy rests comfortably on his doghouse roof. Yes, he wants to be a Tolstoy, a war hero, a world famous lawyer, a hockey instructor, a Don Juan. But Snoopy realizes that he is, after all, a dog, and makes peace with reality. It's okay to be a dog.

So, we conclude, one must adjust to reality or suffer the consequences of a negative character trait. But that does not mean that we must forever deprive ourselves of the pleasures of fantasy. We just have to be careful that we are not carried away by fantasy, and we must return to the real world, just like Snoopy does.

As I mentioned earlier, a vacation is often a break with one's reality, but it is a healthy break. A fishing or skiing trip, or spending time on a ranch may be a welcome respite from the stresses of reality. Let us enjoy our vacations to the fullest, and we can then deal more effectively with the drudgery of reality when we return. In fact, reality does not have to be the drudgery we often make it. We can find things to be happy about if we just look for them, and of course, we can also enjoy vacation when it becomes a reality.

*Peanuts*® by Charles M. Schulz. Reprinted by permission of United Features Syndicate, Inc.

Lucy is not right. When my little girl once refused to finish her vegetables, my wife reprimanded her, "Think of the children who are starving in Ethiopia, who don't have any food on their plate." My daughter responded, "And if I eat the vegetables, will the children in Ethiopia feel better?"

There is indeed much misery in the world, but if I refuse to take or enjoy a vacation, would that eliminate all the misery? Of course not. So as Snoopy does, be sensible. Get back to the realities of the world when you return from your vacation. But today, during the vacation, laugh and dance and enjoy it.

# Chapter 3

# Reminders of Reality

One of the techniques of psychotherapy that has proven itself to be very valuable is group therapy. Some psychological problems that are resistant to even intensive, long term, one-to-one therapy may be resolved when a group of people seeking self-awareness work together, with and "on" each other, facilitated by a therapist.

One of the advantages of group therapy is that while a person may be oblivious to some of his own problems or hang-ups, he may be very astute in observing these very same traits in other people. What may happen in a group is that Jim is blind to his own hang-ups, but can see them in Bob and Betty and Jean and Joe. They, in turn, are each blind to their own emotional quirks, but can see them in others. In ongoing group sessions, various psychological problems can be flushed out, brought out in the open for discussion, and may be ultimately recognized and re-solved. The fact that Jim has hang-ups of his own still allows him to be a very valuable observer of Joe, and he may help Joe appreciate and deal with his reality, and vice versa. What often happens is that members with similar negative character traits help each other.

So here we have Woodstock, a little canary that, like Snoopy, has a fantasy. Yet Woodstock serves as a reality check to Snoopy, because Woodstock does not "buy into" Snoopy's fantasies, and can punch holes in them, keeping Snoopy grounded. Woodstock can therefore serve as "Sancho Panza" when Snoopy becomes Don Quixote. By the same token, when Woodstock gets lost in fantasy land, Snoopy can bring him back to reality.

*Peanuts*® by Charles M. Schulz. Reprinted by permission of United Features Syndicate, Inc.

Snoopy may be hoping to be part of a family as big and heroic as the St. Bernard's, but does he know whether it is a dream or not? What is reality and what is fantasy? Daydreamers, in general, don't have a tendency to be unrealistic, particularly those who can generally distinguish between the two. But sometimes the margins are blurred. Reality may be confused with what we wish it to be. That is, we think something is real because we would want it to be that way. But our wishes may be only wishes, and reality may not comply with them. For the person who has a consistent habit of being out of touch, or living in a dream world, the pattern of thinking is severe.

Sometimes one of two people in a relationship gets carried away by fantasy, but the other anchors onto reality. If the second is swept away by fantasy, problems may arise. For example, a husband who fantasizes that he earns much more than he does may be held in check by his wife who has a good grasp on reality. If she, too, begins to believe in his fantasy, they may soon find themselves deeply in debt, as they both spend much more than they have.

Snoopy tries to convince Woodstock that his desire to find his mother is most unrealistic. But what happens? Snoopy gets carried away and thinks he has found *his* mother. In other words, Snoopy now adopts Woodstock's fantasy.

Snoopy's distortion of reality is quite extreme. How could someone possibly mistake a St. Bernard for a beagle? The answer is that when there is a need for rationalizing, one rationalizes, regardless of how far out it may be. So it ends up that Snoopy justifies his fantasy, while still being critical of Woodstock as being unrealistic.

Woodstock's grasp on reality is often better than Snoopy's, much to Snoopy's disappointment. Woodstock has come to take everything Snoopy says with the proverbial grain of salt.

*Peanuts®* by Charles M. Schulz. Reprinted by permission of United Features Syndicate, Inc.

In the last chapter we saw how Snoopy fails at "being" a snake or a lion. In other strips he has also tried to be a vulture. Of course if someone is in the position of being essentially helpless and totally dependent on a round-headed kid for his survival, it is rather easy to understand why his fantasy might transform him into a formidable and powerful creature. Fantasy is useful then, so long as it is controlled. Snoopy's efforts at being a ferocious hawk might have been a bit more successful, if not for Woodstock's intervention.

*Peanuts*® by Charles M. Schulz. Reprinted by permission of United Features Syndicate, Inc.

Woodstock knows Snoopy's weaknesses and capitalizes on them. Because Snoopy's flawed character trait is not to be particularly realistic about himself, it is easy to convince Snoopy that he will be the guest of honor at a party, where he will stand out like a towering giant over Woodstock's little feathered friends.

Be careful when people titillate your ego. You may be in for the shock of your life.

*Peanuts®* by Charles M. Schulz. Reprinted by permission of United Features Syndicate, Inc.

Often we have seen Snoopy imagine himself an enchanting lover, even though his letters overtly betray the superficiality and capriciousness of his affection, even though there is no significant other in his life.

*Peanuts®* by Charles M. Schulz. Reprinted by permission of United Features Syndicate, Inc.

Snoopy must think that his love letters will cast a spell over his wished-for beloved. While Snoopy indulges in this fantasy, Woodstock recognizes the letters for what they really are.

*Peanuts*® by Charles M. Schulz. Reprinted by permission of United Features Syndicate, Inc.

Families of unrealistic people often wonder whether they should humor the person and go along with his unrealistic notions or should challenge his false beliefs. After all, a family might think, these are not psychotic beliefs we're referring to; the unrealistic person is just hurting himself by not dealing with the ins and outs of life. He may react violently when disagreed with, so family members may therefore think it is better to go along with these notions, especially when doing so does not appear to be harmful in any way. As a rule, this is a mistake. We must live in reality, and regardless of how difficult acceptance of reality may be, we must adjust to it, unless, of course, we are capable of changing it to better suit us. Agreeing with the person's fantasies only reinforces them, and makes it more difficult for the person to relinquish them and live in the real world.

*Peanuts®* by Charles M. Schulz. Reprinted by permission of United Features Syndicate, Inc.

Snoopy chose the easy way, to play along with Woodstock's fantasies. But the easy way is often not the best way, and even at the risk of incurring someone's displeasure, one should stay with the truth.

Snoopy does not always go along with Woodstock's fantasies. Sometimes he stands up to him, even then he may yield a bit, perhaps to avoid completely offending his little feathered friend.

*Peanuts®* by Charles M. Schulz. Reprinted by permission of United Features Syndicate, Inc.

Sometimes we are unaware that some of our behavior we believe to be based on stark, undeniable reality is actually based on a kind of fantasy. There is a danger in this, because when fantasy of any kind replaces reality, the quality of life is bound to be adversely affected.

Clinically we see this in instances where children have to assume adult roles in childhood. This is likely to happen in dysfunctional families, where for one reason or another, one or both parents are derelict in their roles, resulting in one of the children becoming a stand-in father or mother.

Sometimes the adoption of a parental role in childhood can be sublimated fairly constructively, as when a child who was the caregiver in the family grows up to be a doctor, nurse, teacher, or social worker, thereby continuing the role assumed in childhood. Even when this occurs, however, there may be undesirable consequences, especially when the caregiver feels that his or her only raison d'être is to care for others, and totally neglects himself or herself in the process.

One woman I treated went into a profound depression which proved resistant to all treatment. Her history revealed that as a child she had assumed many of the maternal chores and duties in her family because her mother had become dysfunctional. Many years later her younger siblings referred to her as "our real mother."

*Peanuts*® by Charles M. Schulz. Reprinted by permission of United Features Syndicate, Inc.

When her own children grew up and left home, she still had her husband to care for. When he died she was left without anyone to look after, and although she had adequate means to live comfortably and even to travel around the world, she retreated into a shell, and even intensive psychiatric treatment could not alleviate her depression. The reason? Her cause for existence had disappeared. She valued herself only as someone who could care for others, and when there was no longer anyone to care for, she lost all will to live. She had bought into the fantasy that she was "the real mother" for everyone and with no separate life for herself. When this function was over for her, her raison d'être was gone.

We must be careful how we structure our lives. The lack of a grasp on who we really are inside is a negative trait. Perhaps even more important, we should encourage our children to develop healthy identities. It is certainly important to teach children to help others who are in need, but we must be careful that they do not lose themselves, their grounding, as they do so.

Early in this chapter we spoke of group therapy. Another valuable feature of group therapy is that many people may be oblivious to their personality strengths and assets, as well as their flaws, and may suffer from unwarranted low self-esteem. They may make a niche for themselves in life, and based on a distorted self-perception, relegate themselves to a role far beneath their actual potential.

The tragedy is that a person may spend an entire lifetime in that kind of role simply because he is unaware of his potential. At best, this deprives the world of contributions that he could have made. At worst, this may lead to personal dissatisfaction and complications such as alcoholism, drug addiction, unhappy marriages, and any of a variety of psychosomatic illnesses. So, a fantasy that puts us in an inferior place is equally as destructive as grandiose thinking.

Strangely enough, a crisis, such as that precipitated by alcoholism, may be a blessing in disguise, because it may jolt a person into a search for the self that has been concealed. It is unfortunate that it may take a life crisis to arouse the person from his state of lethargy. How wonderful it would be if this enlightenment could occur without the pain of a crisis.

*Peanuts*® by Charles M. Schulz. Reprinted by permission of United Features Syndicate, Inc.

Like Snoopy, we have always a chance of doing something to improve ourselves, whether physically by exercising our muscles, or psychologically and spiritually by eliminating character defects and strengthening our spirituality. But like Snoopy, many of us prefer to take the path of least resistance. Perhaps we cannot achieve the absolute tranquillity that Snoopy does lying atop his doghouse, but we can certainly be guilty of trying to avoid anything we might have to work at that would disturb our composure.

Like Snoopy, many of us hope that a crisis will never occur. Although understandable, this is really not the best course, because without a crisis, we are unlikely to change the status quo, unless, of course, someone makes us aware that we are in a rut, and stimulates us to escape it. Laziness of character is bound to put us in a rut.

This is where a true friendship or a relationship with a mentor, such as a spiritual advisor can be one's salvation. This person puts us to work on our deficiencies. He or she can alert us to our untapped potential and our true identity that lies concealed somewhere within us, waiting to be discovered.

*Peanuts*® by Charles M. Schulz. Reprinted by permission of United Features Syndicate, Inc.

Yes, Snoopy is in there somewhere, and Woodstock could help him find himself—the real Snoopy. Woodstock could help him give his character a push. But Snoopy closes his eyes and drifts off to sleep rather than look for the grounded, concealed self, the one that's not flawed. Alas, like Snoopy, we too often choose to abandon the search for our real selves, and rest comfortably in our niche.

There is a folk saying that "the worm that infests the horseradish thinks there is no sweeter place in the world." Horseradish root is bitter. Why would the worm choose so bitter a vegetable when there is an abundance of sweeter vegetables? The wisdom of the folk saying is that since the worm has not experienced anything sweeter, he must think that the horseradish is the best available in the world.

So it often is with ourselves. We may adapt to a particular role and status in life, in the belief that this is all there is. We may be like an uncut diamond, whose scintillating beauty is within, but not visible until the outer layers are removed. If we work at discovering ourselves, we will be pleasantly surprised.

Chapter 4

# A Tale of Two Sisters: When Someone Has to Be the Boss

There are various ways of categorizing people. These classifications are not exclusive, and one person may fit into any number of categories. One way of dividing people is into "passive" versus "assertive" categories. Some people are more domineering, while others allow themselves to be dominated. Some people are leaders, others are followers.

Some people push themselves into positions of leadership, and may achieve their authority by means of brute force, as is often the case with dictators. On the other hand, natural-born leaders are often reluctant to assume positions of authority, and may be catapulted into these roles by people who recognize their qualities of leadership and who wish to be led by them. While both kinds of leaders exhibit leadership qualities as a character trait, the first type possesses a negative one. They are generally insecure in their positions, knowing that they have to forcibly impose their will on others, and because they feel insecure, they continually seek to reinforce their dominance. The second type can govern with greater serenity, secure in the knowledge that they have the confidence of the people.

Patterns of dominance may vary. Lucy is older than Linus, and takes advantage of her seniority in order to exert absolute dominance. Sally, who is younger than Charlie Brown, does indeed dominate him, but in this case the relationship is primarily due to Charlie Brown's willingness to be dominated. Let us look at some of these differences.

*Peanuts*® by Charles M. Schulz. Reprinted by permission of United Features Syndicate, Inc.

Lucy exerts her authority by means of brute force. Linus's appeal for justice and for respect of his rights have no effect whatsoever.

The world of children often reflects the world of adults. We may note, incidentally, that Schulz tells us much about adult psychology, even though no adult ever appears in his comic strip.

Nations also have character traits. Anyone observing the relationships of nations and international politics can easily see through the facade of "agreements" among nations, purportedly arrived at through rational negotiation, and can realize that powerful nations intimidate lesser nations, and invariably get what they want.

Stronger nations enter into these agreements with weaker nations in which they may state that they merely wish it to govern more effectively, to everyone's advantage, and really do not wish to dominate anyone. But history proves this is not so. Lucy suggests such an agreement, but we know Lucy too well to be taken in.

*Peanuts*® by Charles M. Schulz. Reprinted by permission of United Features Syndicate, Inc.

The agreements between two nations may appear to be fair on paper, but when they are implemented in reality, the story is considerably different. This is true of nations, of siblings, and in industry and commerce as well.

*Peanuts*® by Charles M. Schulz. Reprinted by permission of United Features Syndicate, Inc.

The need to dominate someone smaller or weaker is a trait we should address in ourselves. A stronger nation or company that wishes to maintain its authority may dismiss any appeals for fairness or equality and exert its control by either overt or covert threat. The same, unfortunately, is true of dominating people.

*Peanuts*® by Charles M. Schulz. Reprinted by permission of United Features Syndicate, Inc.

It is not unusual for the weaker party to try and flex its muscles. Think of nations that have sought to break away from the dominating power.

*Peanuts*® by Charles M. Schulz. Reprinted by permission of United Features Syndicate, Inc.

Throughout history, there have been kings who ruled by Divine Right. While some might not explicitly state that they have been commanded by God to rule the world, they nevertheless may believe in a "manifest destiny," that is both their right and obligation to dominate others. The same principle holds true for "civilians."

*Peanuts®* by Charles M. Schulz. Reprinted by permission of United Features Syndicate, Inc.

CEOs and other authority figures may act no differently than older siblings or dictatorial governments. Sometimes they may fly into an irrational rage if they feel that their honor was offended. I was once in the presence of the head of a department at a university, when a graduate student approached him with a question. The man did not even let the student finish the question, interrupting him with an angry reprimand, "Don't you know protocol?" meaning that the student should have gone through appropriate channels rather than approaching the mighty one directly. He seemed no more than a bully, surely an unnecessary trait in a man of his renown.

*Peanuts*® by Charles M. Schulz. Reprinted by permission of United Features Syndicate, Inc.

I thought the chief of the department was a jerk. His attempt to defend his honor did not elevate my esteem of him. In a position of authority, people will respect you more if you do not, like Lucy, expect to be saluted. Only those in power who unfortunately have a "weak link" in their personality need abeyance.

Some governments insist that they do not suppress freedom of speech, and claim that the press and electronic media are free to say whatever they wish. That is, if the media just happens to support the position of the party in power. The chairman of the board of a corporation may deny that he has surrounded himself with "yes men." That everyone happens to get along with the chairman's opinion is just because they see the wisdom of it.

*Peanuts*® by Charles M. Schulz. Reprinted by permission of United Features Syndicate, Inc.

Some nations have been so bludgeoned into servility that they have become totally self-effacing and have lost their identity. We often see this in marriages where there is spousal abuse, either physical or emotional, or in abusive parent-child relationships, where the child never develops a sense of identity for fear of offending a bullying parent.

*Peanuts*® by Charles M. Schulz. Reprinted by permission of United Features Syndicate, Inc.

Of course, there is always the possibility that smaller nations might grow and develop into powers that might eventually challenge the superpower. The same is true of people. The latter may therefore try to suppress such growth.

This pattern is ancient indeed, and can be found all the way back to biblical times, when the King of Egypt said of the Hebrews "Come let us get wise to them, lest they increase, and should we be attacked by an enemy, they will join forces with them." They therefore put harsh task masters over the Hebrews, in order to suppress them with hard labor. (Exodus 1:10–11).

Dominant powers and people may try to suppress their subjects through deprivation of sustenance, freedom of thought, alienating or isolating them, and physical brutality. Whatever the method, and however disguised and rationalized, the purpose is all the same.

*Peanuts*® by Charles M. Schulz. Reprinted by permission of United Features Syndicate, Inc.

Nations, much like individuals, can be intimidated in ways other than by brute force or oppression. Smaller nations can be made to feel totally inadequate, inept, and unable to survive on their own, that they need protection by the superpower. They may become convinced of their dependency on the superior force, which can then become paternalistic and assert that it has greater wisdom in providing for the needs of the smaller nations.

Let us get back to our two sisters. In contrast to Lucy, who is older than Linus and can dominate him by force, Sally is younger than Charlie Brown, but she manipulates him, taking advantage of his feelings of inadequacy to assert herself. Sally knows Charlie's weak spots and how to push his buttons. She can deflate Charlie on the one hand, then use this position of strength to manipulate him to do her homework.

Sally, being a younger sister, cannot exert the brute force that Lucy does. Instead, she has an extensive armamentarium of techniques whereby she gets her older brother to do her bidding. Again, if we are alert, we may detect a bit of ourselves in this relationship.

*Peanuts*® by Charles M. Schulz. Reprinted by permission of United Features Syndicate, Inc.

It might seem to be an internal contradiction, in that Sally turns to Charlie for help because she recognizes he is in fact smarter than she, yet she knocks him as being ignorant. As illogical as it may be, conflicting ideas are commonplace in human relations, as any observer of politics can attest.

In contrast to Lucy, who never has a kind word to say about anyone, Sally can also get things done for her by flattery. It is not difficult to think of people who lavish praise on others and even smother them with compliments because they wish to exploit them. The often-heard adage "Flattery will get you nowhere" is simply not true. People who are hungry for feelings of worthiness are especially vulnerable to positive strokes, whether sincere or not.

*Peanuts®* by Charles M. Schulz. Reprinted by permission of United Features Syndicate, Inc.

Using force or manipulation to dominate another is an aspect, and not a nice one, of character. Another powerful tool for control is guilt. Guilt is a very distressing feeling, and it is because we wish to avoid the misery of guilt that we forego many pleasures. Some parents try to control their children's behavior with guilt: "If you do that, I'll have a heart attack," or "You are killing me." Inducing guilt in another is hurtful. Because guilt is so painful, it can be used to manipulate people, and Sally is a pro at this.

*Peanuts*® by Charles M. Schulz. Reprinted by permission of United Features Syndicate, Inc.

There are reasons why a particular person is more vulnerable to being manipulated. In *I Didn't Ask to Be in This Family* (1996), Charlie Brown, who feels crushed by his repeated failures, such as his perennial losing streak of baseball games or being the butt of his friends' jibes, has a temporary respite when Sally is born. Being an older brother gives him a feeling of status that he had never previously experienced. Furthermore, his parents give him the responsibility of caring for Sally. Charlie develops feelings of indebtedness to Sally for making him feel better, as well as feelings of responsibility, which render him exquisitely susceptible to her machinations. It does not take much for Sally to wrap Charlie Brown around her little finger.

*Peanuts®* by Charles M. Schulz. Reprinted by permission of United Features Syndicate, Inc.

Eventually, Sally's taking advantage of Charlie Brown's weakness works against her, which is usually what happens when we put our negative character traits to work. If we can identify with either Sally as the manipulator or as Charlie Brown as being a subject of manipulation, we may be able to take corrective action, since neither of these traits are to our advantage.

In *Life's Too Short* (1995), I pointed out that many types of behavior represent attempts to cope with feelings of low self-esteem. Schulz is a master at illustrating some of this behavior, not only of our two sisters but also, of course, Charlie Brown, who never fights against his feelings of inadequacy. He simply surrenders to them. Lucy, however, reacts with an attitude of grandiosity, arrogance, and self-righteousness.

It is characteristic of people like Sally, who may not do much of anything, to emphasize whatever they *can* do, hoping to make up in quantity for what is lacking in quality. And to quit while they are ahead.

*Peanuts*® by Charles M. Schulz. Reprinted by permission of United Features Syndicate, Inc.

I heard a story about a preacher who once left the text of his sermon on the lectern. One of the worshippers noted that there were various comments in the margins, indicating what rhythm or tone of voice to use at different parts. At one point there was a note that read, "Argument awfully weak here. Yell like hell."

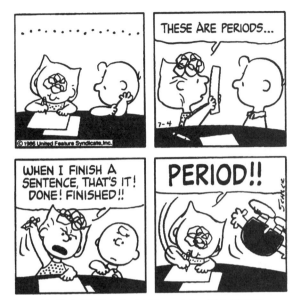

*Peanuts*® by Charles M. Schulz. Reprinted by permission of United Features Syndicate, Inc.

Perhaps Sally cannot write an essay, but she makes certain that her periods are plentiful and emphatic, an outgrowth of her need to compensate for her inability to commit real substance to the page.

It is not unusual for manipulative people to also hedge a bit on the truth. Once a person has decided to seek the easy way out, cuts on ethics are often taken, and one can always rationalize whatever one does. This is how using one negative aspect of character puts us in danger of using another and another.

This, however, is too much for Charlie Brown, who is as straight as a wire, and this is one situation in which the meek Charlie Brown becomes assertive. It takes all the courage he can muster, but he cannot let his sister become corrupt.

*Peanuts*® by Charles M. Schulz. Reprinted by permission of United Features Syndicate, Inc.

Charlie Brown teaches us that to keep silent in the face of wrongdoing is actually condoning it. Also he shows that confronting his own character trait helps him improve. Thank you, Mr. Schulz!

Consistent with the traits of manipulativeness and stretching the truth is being too opinionated. Being a "know it all" is a negative character trait. You will find that people who insist that they are right are rather intolerant of other people's opinions, even if those opinions do not affect them in any way, and clearly Schulz knows this. It does not surprise us, therefore, to see how Sally reacts to someone who disagrees with her.

*Peanuts*® by Charles M. Schulz. Reprinted by permission of United Features Syndicate, Inc.

The same intolerance makes forgiving unlikely. If people like Sally for any reason dislike you, don't expect them to accept an apology. They are usually quite obstinate in holding onto resentments toward anyone who displeases them.

*Peanuts*® by Charles M. Schulz. Reprinted by permission of United Features
Syndicate, Inc.

They are also likely to dissemble and behave hypocritically.

*Peanuts®* by Charles M. Schulz. Reprinted by permission of United Features Syndicate, Inc.

In contrast to neuroses, which, as we pointed out, are disorders that affect only part of the personality, a character trait is more like an integral part of the personality. Thus, while neuroses may come on at any time in a person's life, character traits are often noticeable at an early age, and may not undergo much change throughout one's life. This gives rise to the colloquial aphorism, "Just as one is at seven, that's how he is at seventy." Which is why we have to work so hard to change the "bad" ones.

Schulz shows us how Sally was when she was just a tot. Even then she sought to evade anything that she thought might inconvenience her, and tried to enlist Charlie Brown's help to extract her from any situation. People like Sally frequently ask for letters from doctors, for example, to exempt them from gym, or anything else that they would rather not do. They are no different when they grow up than they were as children.

*Peanuts®* by Charles M. Schulz. Reprinted by permission of United Features Syndicate, Inc.

By the same token they are intolerant of others who share one or two similar traits: One person who evades income taxes may be self-righteous in criticizing someone else who seeks exemption from duty, and may even demand that he be dealt with harshly.

*Peanuts®* by Charles M. Schulz. Reprinted by permission of United Features Syndicate, Inc.

Manipulation is frequently counterproductive. There may indeed be a short-term gain, but since this usually results in not doing for oneself what one should be doing, the long-term results are invariably negative.

For example, Sally tries to get Charlie Brown to do her homework for her, and is willing to accept anything he writes as long as it will relieve her of this chore.

*Peanuts*® by Charles M. Schulz. Reprinted by permission of United Features Syndicate, Inc.

One poorly reasoned act is for students to copy others' work or even cheat on an exam in order to get a good grade. These "good grades" do not increase their knowledge a single bit. Later, when they need the information they did not learn, the spurious A on the record will not compensate for their ignorance. Sally, too, misses the whole point; namely, that the purpose of school and homework is to learn something.

*Peanuts®* by Charles M. Schulz. Reprinted by permission of United Features Syndicate, Inc.

But is it possible that Sally does not know that one goes to school in order to learn?

This is where the powerful psychological defense mechanism of denial comes into play. The real reason Sally shuns homework is because she is lazy, simply lazy, which makes her rationalize and dismiss school as unimportant.

Because Sally's domination over Charlie Brown is not as absolute as that of Lucy over Linus, Sally must resort to a variety of techniques. We have already seen that she uses flattery and guilt to control Charlie. Another common trait, which we unwittingly use in many relationships is bribery. While bribery is illegal in sports, law, and government, it is quite common in relationships.

*Peanuts®* by Charles M. Schulz. Reprinted by permission of United Features Syndicate, Inc.

As we noted earlier, some people are more assertive and aggressive than others. We therefore cannot say that there is anything abnormal about being dominant. Some people are leaders, while others are followers. At what point, though, does a trait cease to be normal and become pathologic?

In a healthy leader-follower relationship, both parties are generally content with their respective roles. When followers feel oppressed by the leader, the likelihood is that the dominating trait is unhealthy. This is quite obvious in a dictatorship, where although the populace may gather to salute the despotic leader, even cheering wildly for him, they may loathe him with a passion. His oppressiveness may take the joy out of life, yet one must feign happiness. Oppressed people are required to sing the leader's praises out of fear, but there is little doubt as to their true feelings.

Authoritarian governments are always touting how everyone in their country is blissful. Elections in these countries are usually uncontested and result in a one-hundred percent vote of confidence for the party in power. People who live under the domination of a dictator have no choice but to proclaim that they are satisfied.

*uts® by Charles M. Schulz. Reprinted by permission of United Features Syndicate, Inc.

True and good leaders have their followers' best interests at heart. They provide guidance and, where appropriate, constructive criticism. Discipline of a nation, as well as of a child, may sometimes require imposing restrictions, but like a devoted parent, a benevolent leader takes no pleasure in doing so, and issues restrictive edicts only when absolutely essential. The power-hungry leader, on the other hand, will exert his authority anywhere and everywhere, and may actually seek out ways in which to oppress the populace.

*Peanuts®* by Charles M. Schulz. Reprinted by permission of United Features Syndicate, Inc.

Finally, pathological dominance is often characterized by frank sadism. The despotic leader not only inflicts unnecessary suffering on the populace but actually delights in doing so. History is not at a loss for such sadistic rulers.

On a smaller scale, this can be true of any superior/subordinate relationship. Parent-child, husband-wife, teacher-student, employer-employee, and in any other relationship where one person can wield power over another. All such relationships provide a potential for abuse. Sadistic dominance is clearly a pathological trait.

The difference between our two sisters, Lucy and Sally, is also evident in their romantic lives. While both young women are rather aggressive in pursuit of their men, there is just no comparison between Lucy's overbearing attitude, which is sure to be self-defeating, and Sally's more assertive, positive, modus operandi. Thus, the attitudes that Lucy and Sally manifest within their families are evident in their relationship to others outside the family.

Sally has a crush on Linus, whom she calls her "sweet Babboo." Even though Linus does not confirm her perception that he is in love with her, she is merely suggesting it, and is not overbearing.

*Peanuts*® by Charles M. Schulz. Reprinted by permission of United Features Syndicate, Inc.

This is quite different from Lucy's approach to Schroeder, which is virtually terrorizing, and is hardly likely to elicit any tender feelings. Lucy insists that she is attractive, hence Schroeder must be madly in love with her, although Schroeder certainly does not see it that way.

Fully aware of Schroeder's worship of Beethoven, Lucy assumes that her charms will triumph over his formidable competitor, which only incites Schroeder's fury to have his idol so belittled.

Unperturbed, Lucy continues to relentlessly pressure Schroeder, upping the ante, so to speak, becoming more aggressive, which only results in his categorically rejecting her. This is where Lucy's defense mechanisms kick in. When one is confronted with intolerable thoughts, denial comes into play. Schroeder's emphatic rejection does not have a significant impact on Lucy, who simply dismisses his unequivocal rejection.

*Peanuts*® by Charles M. Schulz. Reprinted by permission of United Features Syndicate, Inc.

Between Sally and Lucy we have two varieties of attempted subjugation. We shall soon see what may be responsible for such traits.

# Chapter 5

# Lucy: How Great It Is to Be Perfect!

Let us smile and enjoy Lucy to the utmost, because it is only in a comic strip that we can do so. Real-life Lucys are not in the least bit amusing. They are quite obnoxious, and we tend to keep our distance from them. Most probably Lucy's overbearing behavior is born out of her feelings of low self-esteem.

Lucy is arrogant, opinionated, self-righteous, and all the other things that we associate with people who believe that they are the center of the universe. What we may not recognize is that this grandiosity is invariably a defense against profound feelings of inferiority and unworth.

Lucy? Feelings of inferiority and unworth? You must be kidding.

No. Lucy's traits are a desperate defense, because Lucy is nothing other than the mirror image of Charlie Brown. Whereas Charlie Brown feels he is nothing, Lucy defends against her own similar feelings by asserting that she is everything. The validity of this theory is established in a strip in which Lucy asks Schroeder, "Do you think I'm beautiful?" and for once he says, "I think you're the most beautiful girl the world has ever known," to which Lucy responds, "You hate me, don't you?" Many people are disagreeable when they are told that they are right.

*Peanuts*® by Charles M. Schulz. Reprinted by permission of United Features Syndicate, Inc.

Lucy's grandiosity can thus be seen as a defense against her feelings of inferiority. When Schroeder tells her she is indeed very beautiful, she no longer needs her defenses, and her true feelings about herself emerge.

But such moments of truth are few and far between. Lucy's arrogance alienates people, which only intensifies her feelings of unworth, to which she reacts with more grandiosity, in a self-perpetuating cycle. Lucy's grandiosity is not feigned. She sincerely believes she is perfect, but this belief is actually rooted in a self-deprecation of which she is not conscious. The same may be true of ourselves if we have this trait, though we may not be able to recognize it.

Those of us who accept our fallibility as mere mortals can usually accept constructive criticism more or less gracefully. Indeed, this may help us improve ourselves, which will result in lesser grounds for any further criticism. If, however, we insist that we are right and project blame onto everyone and everything else, we are likely to continue making mistakes, which will invite more criticism. Again, this is a vicious cycle.

Peanuts® by Charles M. Schulz. Reprinted by permission of United Features Syndicate, Inc.

The defensive nature of Lucy's grandiosity is quite transparent. She projects when she cannot hit the ball, and she projects when she does not catch the ball. Just as it is her failures that make her project so it is her feeling of being defective that results in her grandiosity.

Lucy goes even beyond exonerating herself by placing the blame on others. It is classic of a practicing alcoholic to insist that all his obvious mistakes are actually stunning successes which no one else seems to appreciate, but this is hardly restricted to alcoholics. Just look around and see how many people who goofed are insistent that what they did was absolutely right! She even has the audacity to claim that her failure was a success!

*Peanuts®* by Charles M. Schulz. Reprinted by permission of United Features Syndicate, Inc.

It takes more than just a bit of audacity to claim she was right when she threw the ball to the wrong base.

During the height of the domestic conflict about the Vietnam War, one of the parties arguing for escalation of the war said that the United States had never lost a war, and that we must preserve this noble record at all costs. One senator (as reported in the Congressional Record) saw this as no obstacle to a U.S. pullout. "Let Congress pass a resolution that we won the war and then pull out," he said. But how could we claim victory when we were suf-

fering unprecedented casualties? How can you claim to be win-
ning when you are losing? Well, Lucy could!

*Peanuts*® by Charles M. Schulz. Reprinted by permission of United Features Syndicate, Inc.

It might appear at first glance that Lucy is self-confident. She
seems to have no doubt that she will mature into a stunningly
beautiful woman.

*Peanuts®* by Charles M. Schulz. Reprinted by permission of United Features Syndicate, Inc.

Self-confident people do not go around making statements that project that they "know it all." A person who feels competent will assume that others will become aware of their competence. It is the person who lacks self-confidence that usually acts like a "know-it-all," and who can make the most absurd statements . . .

*Peanuts*® by Charles M. Schulz. Reprinted by permission of United Features Syndicate, Inc.

. . . and fabricate facts to suit themselves.

*Peanuts*® by Charles M. Schulz. Reprinted by permission of United Features Syndicate, Inc.

Lucys are not people we enjoy having around, and in fact, we try to avoid them because of their overbearing attitude and caustic comments.

The arrogance of the Lucys among us alienates many people, but they seek to blame this on everything except their personality. Here Charlie Brown tries to help explain away her alienation.

*Peanuts®* by Charles M. Schulz. Reprinted by permission of United Features Syndicate, Inc.

Charlie Brown was not of much help to Lucy. In fact, such "helpful" reassurance only reinforces the person's pathology. However, look what happens if somebody does tell Lucy the truth! No wonder people tend to humor her.

*Peanuts®* by Charles M. Schulz. Reprinted by permission of United Features Syndicate, Inc.

My interpretation that Lucy's grandiosity is defensive rather than genuine is further validated by observing Lucy's moods. If Lucy were really convinced about how great a person she is, she would be happy. But Lucy is anything but happy. Lucy is a grouch who blames her attitude on being born with "crabby genes." In fact, Lucy doesn't even know how to smile anymore, which is hardly what one would expect of a person who is really happy with themselves.

*Peanuts®* by Charles M. Schulz. Reprinted by permission of United Features Syndicate, Inc.

No, Lucy is unhappy, primarily because she is really a Charlie Brown at the core. People who do not believe in themselves and are tormented by feelings of inferiority may try to improve their self-esteem by seeing themselves as superior to everyone else around them. In order to do that, though, they have to denigrate everyone else, and indeed, Lucy is constantly deflating others.

*Peanuts*® by Charles M. Schulz. Reprinted by permission of United Features Syndicate, Inc.

In several places Schulz points out that Lucy has a need to deflate others in order to feel better about herself. For example, when Charlie Brown has a temporary rise in self-esteem at the birth of his baby sister, Lucy remarks, "I can think of nothing more obnoxious in this world than a well-adjusted Charlie Brown." Lucy needs Charlie Brown's repeated failures to validate herself. She needs to continually pull away the football to show how inept he is. When Charlie Brown is hospitalized and is unavailable to Lucy as a victim, she feels threatened, and reacts with a near panic.

*Peanuts*® by Charles M. Schulz. Reprinted by permission of United Features Syndicate, Inc.

In spite of her frank arrogance and grandiosity, Lucy contends that she is humble.

*Peanuts*® by Charles M. Schulz. Reprinted by permission of United Features Syndicate, Inc.

If you actually are humble, don't announce it over the public address system. Don't be a Lucy. But on the other hand, don't be a Charlie Brown either. Just get to know yourself, to recognize your strengths and abilities, and try to develop them to their fullest. Respect yourself for who you are, and you will win the respect of others as well.

Chapter 6

# Just Another Thing to Lose At

Charlie is the other side of the coin from Lucy. Anyone interested in problems of low self-esteem will find a gold mine of material in the Charlie Brown character. Charlie loses at everything, but as is characteristic of people with low self-esteem, it is a self-fulfilling prophecy. Charlie Brown loses at baseball primarily because he believes he is going to lose, he falls behind in his schoolwork because he does not make the effort, he gets his kite entangled in the tree because this is what he expects, and he suffers the pangs of unrequited love because he does not have the courage to talk to the little red-haired girl.

Problems related to unwarranted feelings of inferiority and inadequacy are ubiquitous. In *Life's Too Short* (1995), I listed a variety of behaviors that are symptoms of low self-esteem. Charlie Brown has few defense mechanisms to counteract his negative feelings and simply resigns himself to a status of inferiority.

The extremely wide prevalence of low self-esteem makes one wonder about its causes and origins. One might think that such feelings are the result of childhood deprivation and/or abuse, but there is not the slightest indication that Charlie Brown was a victim of abuse or neglect.

*Peanuts®* by Charles M. Schulz. Reprinted by permission of United Features Syndicate, Inc.

One might argue that Lucy's degrading attitude toward Charlie Brown, in which she is joined by several other children, has depressed Charlie Brown's ego. The truth is likely to be just the converse; namely, that Charlie Brown's low self-esteem feelings *invited* the degrading by Lucy and the others. As Eleanor Roosevelt is reported to have said, "No one can put me down except myself."

Charlie Brown's self-effacement is about as extreme as it can get. He thinks of himself as almost nonexistent. Linus champions Descartes's philosophy of *cogito ergo sum,* which means that even if one thinks of himself as not existing, one must nevertheless conclude that one must exist, because if one didn't exist one could not think. Charlie takes this into consideration, but to satisfy Descartes's principle, one need exist only in a most diminutive form, which is what he thinks of himself.

*Peanuts®* by Charles M. Schulz. Reprinted by permission of United Features Syndicate, Inc.

The tenacity with which some people hang onto their image as failures makes one wonder whether some people may not actually feel better with an identity as losers. At one point, Charlie Brown confides to us that he has been reading *The Decline and Fall of the Roman Empire* because he is fascinated by failure.

Why should anyone wish to think of himself as a loser?

People who may not have a positive identity may opt for a negative identity, which they may feel is better than not having an identity at all. The class clown, for example, is usually someone who wishes to draw attention to himself; because he feels he cannot get attention with scholastic excellence, he chooses a negative identity, exercising a negative character trait. Some people may act out in an antisocial manner because that way they can at least achieve an identity, albeit as a criminal. The need for an identity can be so profound that people may take desperate, even self-destructive measures, simply to be a "somebody."

Charlie's assessment is that at best he may be a .0001, so rather than be a nonentity, he chooses an identity as a loser.

*Peanuts*® by Charles M. Schulz. Reprinted by permission of United Features Syndicate, Inc.

This kind of reaction to a negative self-image is an important psychological phenomenon, because it may explain why some people behave in frankly self-destructive ways. For example, a child may act in ways he knows will result in his being punished, and parents may be at their wits' end on how to relate to him. It may just be that if a child has no hope that he can be good, he may decide that he can at least be good at being bad.

Charlie Brown has given up on the possibility of his being good at anything. He simply does not see any possibility that any thing he would do would make people like him.

*Peanuts*® by Charles M. Schulz. Reprinted by permission of United Features Syndicate, Inc.

Is it possible that feelings of inadequacy are actually inborn? While it is generally thought that a person's self-image is the result of one's experiences, or in other words, a learned characteristic, there is reason to consider that some traits as actually being inborn. Observation of infants in the nursery will reveal that there are differences in personalities even among newborns. At any rate, Schulz seems to favor this theory.

Peanuts® by Charles M. Schulz. Reprinted by permission of United Features Syndicate, Inc.

This issue is of more than theoretical significance. Psychological theories that attribute a person's behavior and personality to experiences in early life result in a treatment approach that consists of investigating one's history and trying to correct or undo perceptions that might have been learned early on. If we assume, however, that early life experiences, while no doubt important, are not the primary cause for low-esteem, we can focus more on the here and now and try to help the person cope with his reality rather than to seek an understanding of the origins of his feelings.

There are thus two ways of approaching a psychologically disturbing character trait. One may work from the "inside out," and attempt to understand the origin of the symptom and hope that achieving insight will alleviate the problem. The other way is to work from the "outside in," or try to help a person discard the pathologic behavior, leaving the internal changes to a later time.

Modern-day psychology favors the latter approach, and there is indeed much to be said for it. In my early days of psychiatric practice, when I employed psychoanalytic principles, I had many insightful but neurotic, unhappy patients. When I switched to a more behavior-oriented treatment modality, the results were far better.

For example, I found the Alcoholics Anonymous approach to be much more effective than psychoanalysis for treating many problems, not just substance abuse. Active drinkers who try to explain why they drink are told, "Don't pick up the first drink, and come to meetings," or in other words, "Stop the destructive behavior first, and we'll leave the figuring out why to a later date." The same approach works on clearing up many negative character traits.

One example of acting out feelings of low self-esteem is apparent in the way "wallflowers" behave, those people who just seem to fade into the background; they feel their existence is superfluous. Life for them is drab and meaningless, and it is not unusual for them to escape the distress of ennui by resorting to mind-altering chemicals for thrills. Others may simply resign themselves to this existence, and while they may not get into trouble, neither do they achieve anything of note. Existence is just one huge nothing.

*Peanuts*® by Charles M. Schulz. Reprinted by permission of United Features Syndicate, Inc.

The opposite of those who bemoan their existence are the people who never think about existential issues. They simply move along from birth to death trying to get as much pleasure out of life as they can. They may even be quite happy, much like cows in a pasture who are content with filling their stomachs and resting in the sun. The fact that their lives may have no meaning does not disturb them in the least.

*Peanuts*® by Charles M. Schulz. Reprinted by permission of United Features Syndicate, Inc.

It is different for the person who thinks and who feels that he has no place in this world. He may wonder why it is that he must suffer such a fate. He may search philosophically for some meaning in life . . .

*Peanuts*® by Charles M. Schulz. Reprinted by permission of United Features Syndicate, Inc.

. . . and if he finds no satisfactory answers, he may turn outward in order to identify with some group, such as a cult or a gang, hoping to achieve an identity and feel like he belongs. He may indeed become angry with God for having assigned him so unfair a place in the world. If one was only able to find some reason for his suffering, it might mitigate his distress, but alas! Like Job in the

Scriptures, he may not find anything to explain and justify his suffering, and feel both worthless and purposeless, like a leaf blown about by the wind.

*Peanuts®* by Charles M. Schulz. Reprinted by permission of United Features Syndicate, Inc.

These feelings often pose another threat to people with low self-esteem. They often seek to ingratiate themselves to others, in the hope that by doing favors for others, people will like them. Their sense of self, of identity, however, can only suffer more.

The need to be liked appears to be fundamental to humans, and people who feel that they are unlovable may go to great lengths to achieve a feeling of being wanted. In their solitude they may indulge in grandiose fantasies.

*Peanuts*® by Charles M. Schulz. Reprinted by permission of United Features Syndicate, Inc.

Poor Charlie! He so craves to be loved that he would welcome a hallucination that told him so.

It is little wonder, given how much we all need approval, that some people eschew any kind of behavior that they feel might cause others to reject them. People with good self-esteem may not have any difficulty in doing or saying what they please, but people with low self-esteem are frightened that any negative expression, especially anger, will cause them to be even further alienated, hence they are very restricted in asserting their displeasure.

*Peanuts®* by Charles M. Schulz. Reprinted by permission of United Features Syndicate, Inc.

There is a close correlation between one's self-concept and assertiveness. Of course, when assertiveness is overdone, it may become aggression, which is what we observed in Lucy's behavior. But if someone who has cringed and cowered because of feelings of inferiority can become somewhat assertive, it indicates a favorable change in his psychological makeup.

In my introduction to *When Do the Good Things Start?* (1988), I reflected on whether Charles Schulz is fully aware of the depth of his psychological insights. It is my feeling that like the authors of the great classics, who were probably unaware of the enormity of their intuitive understanding of the human psyche, Schulz, too, writes intuitively, and it is for the reader to grasp the psychological insights in the strips.

For example, in the above strip, Charlie Brown rebukes the tree, stating "You hate me because you need me." It is not at all uncommon to find people who harbor resentments, not toward someone who harmed them, but paradoxically, toward someone who was kind to them. Why? Because some people feel that acknowledging that they are beneficiaries of someone else's kindness would make them beholden or obligated to their benefactor, and because they resent feeling obligated, they develop resentments toward the benefactor.

When I give a talk about the importance of self-esteem, some-one in the audience invariably asks, "What can we do to help our children gain self-esteem?" Among the things that enhance a pos-itive self-image is having one's achievements validated. Parents often "catch" their children doing something wrong, and repri-mand them for it, but when children do the right thing, it is too often taken for granted and not acknowledged. Parents should "catch" their children doing something right, and compliment them for it. This is one way positive character traits are nurtured.

As a word of caution, note that positive strokes have value only when they are genuine. False compliments are worthless, and may be even less because children are very likely to sense that the praise is unjustified, and may come to distrust the parent.

Forget it! Kids know better. It is better to tell your child, "I'm going to play with you, and because I have more experience, I am going to win. But you will watch my moves, and I will show you when the moves you make are unwise. This way you will become a good checkers player."

Historically, Charlie Brown never gets on base, and often strikes out with the bases loaded. But lo and behold, the impossi-ble sometimes happens, and Charlie Brown finds himself on Cloud 9.

*Peanuts*® by Charles M. Schulz. Reprinted by permission of United Features Syndicate, Inc.

However, truth will ultimately prevail. We have come to learn that cover ups are always undone, and when Charlie Brown dis-covers that he was "allowed" to hit the home runs, he is devas-tated.

*Peanuts®* by Charles M. Schulz. Reprinted by permission of United Features Syndicate, Inc.

Charlie Brown wishes that the cover up had been maintained, but that was not to be. The exposure of the sham results in further depression of self-esteem, and in typical Charlie Brown fashion, he retreats to seclusion.

*Peanuts®* by Charles M. Schulz. Reprinted by permission of United Features Syndicate, Inc.

People with low self-esteem are very self-conscious, and are apt to withdraw into seclusion. Because they feel unworthy, they believe that other people will not desire their company and that they will be rejected. They may eliminate the unpleasantness of rejection by avoiding associating with people. It is obvious that if you do not associate with people, they cannot reject you.

Constant self-consciousness is a symptom that something is wrong. You are not aware of your eyes, ears, or throat unless they become diseased.

It is no different with the psyche. An emotionally healthy person is not conscious of the "self" unless he makes an effort to think about himself. However, to be constantly aware of the self is an indication that the self is hurting. Charlie Brown feels so inferior that it hurts, and this results in a self-consciousness.

A person who has a painful pimple on his nose may think that everyone in the world is staring at it. The fact is that no one really notices it and no one cares, but the pain he feels causes him to be so exquisitely self-conscious that he thinks everyone else is as aware of the painful pimple as he is.

Thus, the self-conscious person, who feels himself to be defective and inferior, may believe that everyone notices his defectiveness. He may even think they are talking about him.

*Peanuts®* by Charles M. Schulz. Reprinted by permission of United Features Syndicate, Inc.

Some psychologists theorize that a person with a paranoid personality, who thinks that others are talking about him, is actually desirous of being the object of other people's interest. The thinking goes that because his feelings of unworth and insignificance are so distressing, it gives him a sense of importance to think that others are preoccupied with him.

I am certain that Charles Schulz never read any of these theories, yet he has an intuitive grasp of this phenomenon.

*nuts®* by Charles M. Schulz. Reprinted by permission of United Features Syndicate, Inc.

   While withdrawing from people may eliminate the possibility of being rejected, it comes at the cost of loneliness. The self-conscious person is thus in a dilemma, because it is painful to be with people and painful to be without them. One solution is to live in a large, congested city, where one can be in contact with many people, yet not be in contact with anyone. In some heavily populated cities, people may not know the name of the neighbor who has been living next door to them for the past thirty years. Under such conditions, there is little fear of being rejected, because no one notices you enough nor really cares. While such associations are emotionally sterile, they nevertheless give one the illusion of being part of a group.

*Peanuts*® by Charles M. Schulz. Reprinted by permission of
United Features Syndicate, Inc.

Another aspect of a poor self-image is difficulty in making decisions, which is probably due to a lack of confidence in the capacity to make good judgments.

Because of the inability to trust their own judgments, and in absence of someone who will tell them what they should think, what they should believe, what they should do, these people are tormented by wavering to and fro. Not being certain what is right or is wrong or what they want, they may feel guilty for allowing themselves some pleasure, but on the other hand, if they deny themselves gratification, they may be angry at themselves or at whomever they feel is depriving them of pleasure. They are, in a word, wishy-washy.

*Peanuts*® by Charles M. Schulz. Reprinted by permission of United Features Syndicate, Inc.

Charlie Brown strikes a familiar chord for many people. At one time or another we have probably all felt at least a twinge of inferiority, and many people have felt more than just a twinge. But we are most profoundly touched by Charlie's despair of ever having his fondest wish realized; namely, that the little red-haired girl whom he adores would at least acknowledge his existence, and perhaps even reciprocate his affection.

Charlie Brown is so certain that the chances for any success with the little red-haired girl are hopeless, that he resigns himself to this sad fate, and makes no attempt to realize his dream. Lucy is hardly of any help in encouraging him.

*Peanuts®* by Charles M. Schulz. Reprinted by permission of United Features Syndicate, Inc.

Romance is not the only area where low self-esteem deprives a person of realizing an opportunity. Some people may not apply for a particular job because they feel certain they will be turned down, or submit a manuscript to a publisher because they just know it will be rejected. To a person with good self-esteem, a rejection is indeed painful, yet it is tolerable, and she will take the risk because she realizes that while trying may carry a seventy-five percent risk of rejection, not trying results in one-hundred percent failure.

*Peanuts*® by Charles M. Schulz. Reprinted by permission of United Features Syndicate, Inc.

Poor Charlie! He took the first step toward realizing his dream, but then quickly retreated, thus assuring a failure.

The desire for recognition and acceptance is universal. Some people who suffer from low self-esteem are so certain that they are unlikeable that they make no effort at changing things. While nostalgia is a normal feeling, the past may take on increased importance when there is not much one can anticipate in the future. Perhaps this is why elderly people tend to reflect so much on the past.

Preoccupation with the past can also occur in young people, who, for whatever reason, do not envision much happiness in the future. Another reason for concentrating on the past is that it is a much safer territory for an insecure person who wishes to avoid the risk of making mistakes. One cannot make any new mistakes in the past. Of course, by the same token, one cannot really change history and undo the mistakes of the past. However, fantasy may overpower rationality, and as Charlie Brown says, he would like to "make yesterday better." Lucky for Charlie Brown, for all his unwarranted feelings of inferiority, he nevertheless has some hope that perhaps if he faced up to some of his less likable character traits and made some changes in his personality, he could be liked.

*Peanuts®* by Charles M. Schulz. Reprinted by permission of United Features Syndicate, Inc.

Being aware that one may have a distorted self-image is an important first step in overcoming it, because one may then seek appropriate help in correcting the misconception, consulting a competent therapist.

But beware! Not all psychotherapists are equally adept at treating a low self-esteem problem.

When I attended medical school, I had courses in anatomy, physiology, and biochemistry during the first year, and that was the last of my instruction about normal, healthy human beings. From then on, all my courses, including my training in psychiatry, involved pathology; in other words, a study of diseases rather than a study of health. As a result, I emerged from medical school with a skewed perspective, always looking for the disease in every patient. What is wrong here? Where is the infection? Where is the tumor? Where is the error in metabolism? Where is the mental illness?

Understandably, this must be the primary focus for most medical practitioners. Imagine what it would be like if you consulted a physician for abdominal pain, and after completing the examination, he told you that your eyes, ears, heart, and lungs are in excellent shape. While this may be very reassuring, it is not why you consulted him. You want to know why your abdomen is hurting, and what you can do to get relief. This is not the same when you deal with an emotional illness. Often in these cases the problem is not so much that there is something *wrong* with the patient, as that he is unaware of what is *right* with him. Many of the problems that are brought to the psychotherapist are the result of unwarranted low self-esteem, and are due to a misperception in which the person fails to see his character strengths, and may even be convinced that he has defects that do not exist anywhere except in his imagination. In such cases, it may be a mistake to search for the pathology. Rather, the emphasis should be on helping the person discover and develop his character strengths. Lucy is clearly not the ideal psychotherapist to help a person overcome a low self-esteem problem.

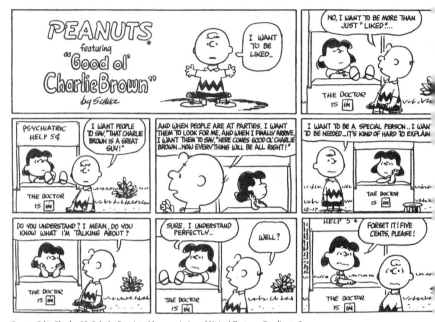

*Peanuts®* by Charles M. Schulz. Reprinted by permission of United Features Syndicate, Inc.

Some people may feel secure and competent in specific areas. For example, a doctor, lawyer, or businessperson may feel very adequate in their particular field of expertise, but may not feel adequate or worthy as a *person*. They may therefore feel very comfortable at the office, where they are confident of their performance, but very uncomfortable at home, where their expertise is of little value, where they must function as a companion or a parent or as a source of emotional support. If they are not confident of their personality assets, they may avoid home, and spend much more time at the office than is actually called for, because this is where they feel most at ease.

Some people, on the other hand, have a global feeling of unworth and inadequacy, and do not feel they have anything going for them in any way.

People with low self-esteem may have difficulty enjoying life because they feel undeserving of pleasure, and they may be afraid to enjoy things or events or relationships because of a foreboding that if they do, it will be taken from them. Some may anticipate that tragedy will strike, and are actually relieved when something bad happens, because they feel that at least for the present, they have suffered sufficiently. Some may actually be driven, probably unconsciously, to precipitate an unpleasant occurrence in order to feel free of an impending disaster.

There is a great deal of interest in methods for coping with stress. Some degree of stress is essential for optimum function, because it stimulates the adrenaline output that alerts and prepares the body to act effectively. It is therefore a mistake to try to avoid all stress, like frequently using alcohol or tranquilizers. Strangely enough, people who lull themselves into inaction with these chemicals may actually deceive themselves to thinking that they are being very productive.

*Peanuts*® by Charles M. Schulz. Reprinted by permission of United Features Syndicate, Inc.

But stress can also be destructive, and an outgrowth of many negative aspects of one's personality is a proclivity to be "stressed out" easily. Too much adrenaline can bring about a state of anxiety that may virtually paralyze a person. And it is a scientific reality that overworrying results in overproduction of adrenaline.

The difference may not be so much in the nature of the stress but rather in how one perceives stress. There is no guarantee that what we do will succeed. We may write a bad exam, fumble a football, or burn the roast. If we perceive failure as an unpleasant occurrence, something we certainly wish to avoid, yet something which we know we can survive, then we may take the stress in stride. If we see failure as being a total devastation that would totally destroy us, then the anxiety level may increase to a counterproductive level.

Obviously, how adequate and secure a person feels about himself is the major determining factor in how he will react to the possibility of failure. Charlie Brown's self-image is so poor that his worry about failure results in his lying awake all night, which in turn is sure to result in a poor performance on the mound the next day. His worry about losing will actually bring about the loss he so fears.

Charlie fantasizes about pitching a no-hitter and hitting home runs, and in spite of his dismal record, never loses hope that a miracle may happen.

Like Snoopy, Charlie Brown occasionally indulges in make believe, hoping to find in fantasy what he despairs of in reality, which could be a great stress reducer except that even his fantasy life is dampened by his poor self-image.

*Peanuts®* by Charles M. Schulz. Reprinted by permission of United Features Syndicate, Inc.

People with low self-esteem may so thirst for recognition that they may be vulnerable to exploitation. While their fantasy may carry them to dizzy heights, they are likely to settle for far less, even for something that is actually demeaning, as long as it calls attention to their existence.

*Peanuts®* by Charles M. Schulz. Reprinted by permission of United Features
Syndicate, Inc.

*Peanuts®* by Charles M. Schulz. Reprinted by permission of United Features
Syndicate, Inc.

Just as there are individual self-concepts, there are also collective self-concepts. These occur especially when we let others define who we are and what we should be like instead of our defining ourselves. A person with a strong, positive self-image may resist being defined by others, but someone who lacks an identity of his own is likely to take on whatever others think is appropriate.

We know that Charlie Brown thinks very little of himself.

*Peanuts®* by Charles M. Schulz. Reprinted by permission of United Features Syndicate, Inc.

Hence when the little red-haired girl moves away and he is deprived of even fantasizing, he cannot allow himself the comfort of crying. Why? Because lacking an individual identity, the only identity that he has is that he is a male. . . .

*Peanuts*® by Charles M. Schulz. Reprinted by permission of United Features Syndicate, Inc.

. . . and to cry would be to lose even that identity.

But let us not leave our Charlie Brown on a sad note. Charlie Brown goes to camp, where he befriends a lonely boy and identifies with him. Having felt the pangs of isolation himself so keenly, Charlie is able to empathize with this boy and help him overcome his loneliness.

Friendship is the magic elixir. A friend can help you enhance
your moments of happiness, and can help assuage suffering and
moments of grief. While receiving friendship is very pleasant, giving of oneself in friendship is even more gratifying. In fact, knowing that he has been of help to someone can even put a smile on
Charlie Brown's face.

*Peanuts*® by Charles M. Schulz. Reprinted by permission of United Features Syndicate, Inc.

# Chapter 7

## Art for Art's Sake

Some people are truly single-minded, totally absorbed in their particular field to the virtual exclusion of everything else. This has given rise to the many stories about absent-minded professors or artists with their heads in the clouds. A favorite story of mine is one about a seminary instructor who was so thoroughly immersed in his theological studies that one day on the way home he could not identify which house was his. He stopped a little girl on the street and asked, "Could you please point out Rabbi C's house to me?" to which the child replied, "Don't you recognize me, daddy?"

To the theologian, the philosopher, the artist, and the musician the entire world may be restricted to the narrow confines of a particular subject. His particular area of interest may take on a sanctity, and he may hallow his subject with a fanatic fervor that surpasses that of the most ardent religious devotee. This can be positive or negative depending on how the person handles his absorption.

Schroeder is such a person. The entire world, nay, the entire universe consists of music, which to him is expressed by the piano, and his idol, Beethoven, whom he reveres no less than a religionist reveres his deity. Just as some believers may wish to convert the entire world to the truth of their particular faith, so Schroeder believes the entire world should recognize the "holiness" of Beethoven. As one who is totally enthralled with the majesty of Beethoven's symphonies, it is not too difficult for me to empathize with Schroeder, although I would hardly parade with a placard.

*Peanuts*® by Charles M. Schulz. Reprinted by permission of United Features Syndicate, Inc.

Many people equate happiness with having whatever they value most. They do not subscribe to the adage "Money cannot buy happiness" because they so value money and material objects that they believe great wealth does assure happiness. As a psychiatrist who has had clinical contact with some very wealthy families, however, I can affirm the truth of the adage. While money may buy many things, it certainly cannot buy happiness.

What does a child think to be the epitome of happiness? Perhaps owning a toy store, where one could play all day and all night with a variety of toys and games. As a child, I was enchanted by train rides, and I used to envy the conductor who rode the train all day. Other children might fancy the proprietor of the sweet shop and ice cream counter to be the luckiest people in the world, because they can have ice cream and candy whenever they so desire.

Alas! There are no guarantees for happiness. Multibillionaires, toy store operators, and ice cream parlor owners, and yes, even train conductors have their share of misery. Schroeder, however, has a hard time believing being Beethoven wouldn't be the answer to anybody's woes.

*Peanuts*® by Charles M. Schulz. Reprinted by permission of United Features Syndicate, Inc.

Relating to a "monolithic" person may have its difficulties. Just as the alcoholic sees nothing of interest in life other than alcohol, and the drug addict sees nothing of worth in anything other than heroin or cocaine, so the monolithic person sees nothing of interest in anything other than his particular field. Any attempt to relate to him in any way other than that which concerns his chosen "totem" is likely to be unsuccessful. Monolithic people may be quite lonely, since others, who cannot communicate with them, may shy away from them. Of course, they may not be conscious of their loneliness since they are thoroughly absorbed in the subject or object they adore.

*Peanuts®* by Charles M. Schulz. Reprinted by permission of United Features Syndicate, Inc.

Hero worshippers are exquisitely sensitive about the object of their adoration and may react with outrage if not outright violence if they feel that their hero's honor has been offended. Such insults have been known to trigger wars between nations.

The reason for this sensitivity may be in the psychology of hero worship. People who have feelings of inferiority or unworthiness, and do not feel that they deserve respect based on their own merit, may try to achieve a feeling of worth by identifying with an object or person that they feel is more deserving of admiration. This ego need is extremely vital, and indeed may be as essential to a person's psyche as oxygen is to his body. An insult to the hero is therefore felt as a direct assault to one's very sense of worth. People who are devotees of a hero may react like Schroeder when he feels the dignity of Beethoven has been challenged.

*Peanuts®* by Charles M. Schulz. Reprinted by permission of United Features Syndicate, Inc.

Identifying with a hero serves yet another purpose: All humans are imperfect. We all make mistakes. Yet there may be desire to reach a state of omniscience or perfection, which is simply not realistic. This hurdle may be overcome by identifying with someone or something that one can conceptualize as being perfect, and by worshipping the perfect object, we share in the perfection. The adoration gratifies the craving for perfection, hence any indication that one's object of worship is defective may be intolerable.

*Peanuts®* by Charles M. Schulz. Reprinted by permission of United Features Syndicate, Inc.

Yes, some artists are indeed interested in money, and may demand a high fee for performing at a concert or an astronomical price for a painting. But there are those who consider money to be a contaminant, and who truly believe in art for art's sake. To them, art is not only priceless but simply cannot be quantified in terms of dollars and cents.

*Peanuts*® by Charles M. Schulz. Reprinted by permission of United Features Syndicate, Inc.

Lucy, who is quite mundane, finds this attitude fascinating. In fact, Lucy's standards are not necessarily based on money. For her, prestige counts even if it depends on various other criteria.

For example, whom does the American culture value the most? The scientist who finds a cure for a life-threatening disease? Hardly. Probably all the scientific awards and salaries of outstanding scientists in the last decade may not equal the annual income of one popular entertainer, whose contributions to the quality of human life may be questionable at best.

*eanuts®* by Charles M. Schulz. Reprinted by permission of United Features Syndicate, Inc.

Let's face it. A brilliant piano virtuoso may not make in an entire lifetime what a star athlete makes in one year. But then again the pianist doesn't have to see his picture on bubble gum cards.

To Schroeder, Beethoven was more than human. Yet when you have an object of worship, he or she does not lose lofty status even if he partakes of mundane pleasures. Just read Greek mythology: the gods were very indulgent, and what they did was simply assign divine status to the pursuit of pleasure, hence the orgies that comprised some forms of ancient religious services. Whatever the gods did must by definition be good; therefore this behavior should be emulated by humans.

*Peanuts*® by Charles M. Schulz. Reprinted by permission of United Features Syndicate, Inc.

To Schroeder, Beethoven did not become less of a super hero because of his passion for macaroni and cheese. In fact, out of reverence for Beethoven, all musicians should love macaroni and cheese (just as some psychoanalysts smoked cigars because Freud did). Lucy, who does not see Beethoven quite in this light, cannot understand why cold cereal is not equally as good.

There are times when Schulz's psychological insights are uncanny. For example, there is a condition known as *anhedonia*, which is the inability to enjoy anything.

Analysis of the sensation of joy reveals that it is invariably the result of the gratification of some desire, as when you are very hungry, you get some tasty food, and enjoy eating. This can be equally true of enjoying a movie, a book, or spiritual experience. Eating without appetite is hardly enjoyable, which is why there are such things as appetizers, to stimulate the desire for food, which serves to enhance the pleasure of eating.

The anhedonic person has no cravings, and life for him is drab and insipid. Some alcoholics have reported that the only thing that stimulated them and enabled them to enjoy anything was alcohol, and that is why they became so dependent on it. Life without pleasure is virtually intolerable.

Schroeder has the desire to be alive, and music stimulates this desire. Poor Charlie Brown, who feels he is doomed to fail at anything, has lost the capacity to look forward to anything. Perhaps anhedonia cannot be referred to as a character trait, but it certainly is an important emotional condition. There are many anhedonic people in the world, many of whom just seem to be carried along by the tide. Many people with anhedonia can be helped psychiatrically, but not, of course, if you have a psychiatrist like Lucy.

A good example of anhedonia is in the story I've heard of two children, the first of whom was put in a room full of toys and was despondent. "If I play with the electric train, I'll probably get a shock and die, and if I play with the construction set, I'll cut my finger and bleed to death," and so on. The second child was put into a room full of manure. He gleefully clapped his hands, exclaiming. "Boy! There must be a pony around here somewhere." The first child is an example of anhedonia.

To Charlie Brown, the repeated failures of life and the inability to anticipate any success have made him anhedonic. Since he feels his cravings will never be satisfied, there is no point in desiring anything, and he does not even have a need to need anymore.

If some of these psychological examples seem farfetched, just wait until you read the next one. It confirms for me how thirty-five years of clinical experience have corroborated Schulz's uncanny insights.

For most of us, the world consists of real objects: people, houses, tables, chairs, cars, and so on. There are also some intangibles, such as music, art, and ideas. We live mostly in the tangible world, while the intangibles provide for our intellectual or aesthetic needs. There are some people for whom the reverse is true; they live mostly in the world of intangibles, which for them is the real world. There are, of course, varying degrees of this condition, but the extreme position is that expressed by the noted philosopher Bishop Berkley's statement, "The world is my idea," by which he meant there is no objective, no concrete reality— only ideas of reality.

One student I've heard about became very involved with Berkley's philosophy, and after hours of profound thinking concluded that Berkley was right, that nothing exists in the outer world, everything is only our idea. Interestingly, once he bumped into a tree, sustaining a terrible blow to his head. His take on this was: "Nothing in the world is real. It is all only an idea, except for that tree."

To some artists, art is the only reality. To Schroeder, music takes on a tangible existence, over and above that it can be heard. It is as though melodies are more than sound waves. In fact, some musicians may think of melodies as having colors and configurations. Even Snoopy can make this happen as when he actually gives music tangibility.

*Peanuts®* by Charles M. Schulz. Reprinted by permission of United Features Syndicate, Inc.

An artist's preoccupation with his art may result in his being quite naive about reality, being able to think only about his subject, and this is where the negative character trait comes in. In college I had a physics instructor who ate, drank, and slept physics. It is said that one time when he was asked his name, he pulled out his slide rule. Knowing the instructor, I would say this story may be more than apocryphal.

This naiveté may make the artist a pushover for manipulators, who may easily sell him the Brooklyn Bridge. Here, Schroeder has to go to camp and is told that there is a plane that will take him there. He joins the children who are pretending while he is dead earnest . . .

*Peanuts*® by Charles M. Schulz. Reprinted by permission of United Features Syndicate, Inc.

. . . and is consequently disappointed when he finds himself still at home.

*Peanuts*® by Charles M. Schulz. Reprinted by permission of United Features Syndicate, Inc.

Some artists are so totally absorbed in their subject that they cannot spare any time or energy for anything else, including love. Schroeder's music can make him totally oblivious to Lucy's very existence, never mind her feelings for him.

*Peanuts*® by Charles M. Schulz. Reprinted by permission of United Features Syndicate, Inc.

When Schroeder does respond to Lucy, it is either with an overt, almost hostile rejection for her detracting him from his playing, or with a more subtle "You go your way and I'll go mine."

*Peanuts*® by Charles M. Schulz. Reprinted by permission of United Features Syndicate, Inc.

Perhaps artists' perfectionism and single mindedness, both traits to admire, may go hand in hand with the gift that drives them. Nothing is more irritating to an artist than comparing his work with something far inferior. A tailor who does custom tailoring may look at off-the-rack clothes with disdain, and a fine cabinet maker may dismiss factory-produced furniture as being junk. But none of these can compare with the rage of a classical music virtuoso, who feels that music has been desecrated by "lesser forms."

*Peanuts*® by Charles M. Schulz. Reprinted by permission of United Features Syndicate, Inc.

Artists can be delightful people, if only you make the effort to understand them. They mean well, and if all they can talk about is their particular subject, let us not be intolerant of them.

*Peanuts*® by Charles M. Schulz. Reprinted by permission of United Features Syndicate, Inc.

# Chapter 8

# Marcie: Ph.D.'s Are Born, Not Made: The Need to Try Harder May Be a Positive

Marcie is your quintessential scholar. She is a dedicated student who makes straight A's. Although dedicated to her studies, Marcie is different than Schroeder, whose only interest in life is classical music. Marcie wishes to engage in other activities, but she is just not adept at them. In contrast to Schroeder, who appears to be a loner, Marcie does make relationships, especially her maternalistic one with Peppermint Patty. Most important, however, is that while Schroeder has no room in his life for love, Marcie does. Nonetheless, Marcie's preoccupation with academic pursuits and her clumsiness in sports might well merit her the appellation of "nerd."

*Peanuts*® by Charles M. Schulz. Reprinted by permission of United Features Syndicate, Inc.

Things that would be a matter of simple common sense, such as not peeling a golf ball, may be beyond the reach of some scholars.

*Peanuts*® by Charles M. Schulz. Reprinted by permission of United Features Syndicate, Inc.

There could be no two greater opposites than Marcie and Peppermint Patty. Each one excels in what the other one fails at. Peppermint Patty is a top athlete, but constantly gets D's, whereas Marcie gets straight A's but has no concept of golf or football.

Although it might seem that the successful scholar is singularly unaffected with the athlete's performance, this is not true. There may be a bit of resentment and envy, as when Marcie feels she must redeem herself for her lack of athletic skill.

*Peanuts*® by Charles M. Schulz. Reprinted by permission of United Features Syndicate, Inc.

Schulz has Marcie constantly addressing Patty as "Sir," which may have two connotations: Marcie may think of Patty, with her athletic prowess, as being rather masculine . . .

*Peanuts*® by Charles M. Schulz. Reprinted by permission of United Features Syndicate, Inc.

or it may be an expression of admiration. Although Marcie is the acknowledged scholar, she considers Patty's athletic skill important. This quite accurately reflects the prevailing attitude. Colleges seem to be much more recognized for the football and basketball teams than for their humanities and sciences departments. A Phi Beta Kappa student may indeed be attractive to recruiters and may get a job offer on graduation, but his salary likely pales in comparison to the athlete who has shown great skill in sports. Does this reflect a collective character trait in society?

Schulz seems to imply that the female intelligencia is not the vanguard of feminism, which as far as I'm concerned is a societal character trait reaching to be addressed again. While Marcie has the data about gender discrimination, it is Peppermint Patty who is aggressive.

*Peanuts®* by Charles M. Schulz. Reprinted by permission of United Features Syndicate, Inc.

While she knows the statistics, Marcie seems to be rather uninvolved in the ramifications of the figures she gives. Perhaps Marcie lacks the assertiveness that an activist must have. Like any other challenge people wish to avoid, Marcie finds a rationalization for her passivity.

*Peanuts*® by Charles M. Schulz. Reprinted by permission of United Features Syndicate, Inc.

Are intellect and emotions mutually exclusive? That is, are highly intellectual people likely to be less sensitive? When I read Thomas Mann's *Magic Mountain*, I asked my professor of psychiatry whether Mann was a physician, since his descriptions of tuberculosis were so accurate. My professor responded, "No way! No physician could have been as sensitive to patients' emotions."

An intellectual person, one who might have a lower perception of sensitivity in others, may take a complaint literally and try to address the problem, unaware that there may be emotional needs behind it.

*Peanuts*® by Charles M. Schulz. Reprinted by permission of United Features Syndicate, Inc.

*Peanuts*® by Charles M. Schulz. Reprinted by permission of United Features Syndicate, Inc.

In caring for someone, it is important that we do not neglect our own needs, for if we do, we may not be of much use to anyone else. This is why flight attendants, when instructing passengers on the use of oxygen, say "If you're traveling with a child, put your own mask on first, and then assist the child." Marcie has gone overboard trying to get Patty to do her book report, but in her diligence to help Patty, Marcie forgets to do her own.

*Peanuts*® by Charles M. Schulz. Reprinted by permission of United Features Syndicate, Inc.

Whereas parental love is usually unconditional and parents have great tolerance, the same cannot be said of Marcie. At one point, Patty exhausts Marcie's patience, and she becomes sarcastic.

*Peanuts®* by Charles M. Schulz. Reprinted by permission of United Features Syndicate, Inc.

It is important to instill self-confidence in others, but this must be based on reality. Marcie's help is not always constructive. Truly sincere people can compliment or criticize without feeling compromised. You may help a person gain self-esteem by focusing on their positive traits, but false praise or flattery is of no value. Marcie would do well to encourage Patty whenever possible, but giving her a false sense of security accomplishes nothing.

# Chapter 9

# Schulz's Gems

We have seen how Peppermint Patty gets poor grades because she fails to do her school work but always finds something or someone else to blame. The reason we so often resort to blame is because we can then rationalize why we do not do those things which we would rather avoid. This negative character trait is at the nest of many human behavior issues.

Take for example, the alcoholic who says, "Of course I drink. What else can I do? My wife constantly nags me about everything, and she just won't let up. If you were married to my wife, you'd drink too."

What he is really saying is, "*I* don't need to change. My *wife* needs to change."

Blaming accomplishes nothing. I believe that psychology has made a grievous error by placing blame on parents for their children's emotional problems. Even if the parents were causative, it does not make the patient any better to place the blame elsewhere. To the contrary, he may wallow in pity: "Poor me. Look how I've been made to suffer. See how they crippled me!

I tell patients who seek to blame their parents, "Even if you are what your parents made you, if you stay that way, it's your own darn fault." Confronting their habit of blame causes many patients to take a giant step forward.

*Peanuts*® by Charles M. Schulz. Reprinted by permission of United Features Syndicate, Inc.

If you really want to improve your life, do something about it. If you wish to stay the way you are but want to be absolved from failure to do anything about it, then go ahead and blame your parents, your schooling, your spouse—whomever.

Sometimes there is nothing you can do about a situation, and then you must try to accept reality with serenity. But trying requires effort. Here, too, the faint of heart (or weak of character) will find someone else to blame in order to relieve them of that chore.

*Peanuts*® by Charles M. Schulz. Reprinted by permission of United Features Syndicate, Inc.

## Denial

"What you don't know won't hurt you." True? Hardly.

Some people would rather be ignorant than know something that greatly displeases them.

*Peanuts®* by Charles M. Schulz. Reprinted by permission of United Features Syndicate, Inc.

## Silence Can Be Golden

Some people seem to think that inasmuch as God gave us the gift of speech, they must use it, even if another solution may be preferable.

Yet the inappropriate use of speech can be disastrous. An untold number of people have been hurt and even killed because of foolish or frankly wicked speech. While withholding comment may also be harmful at times, mankind would often be far better off if people talked less.

Sometimes the correct answer is silence. It is not true that humans are the only creatures that can verbalize. Birds chirp, dogs bark, and cats meow. Each species undoubtedly understands what these vocal expressions mean. The uniqueness of man is not that he can talk but rather that he has the wisdom to know when to keep quiet.

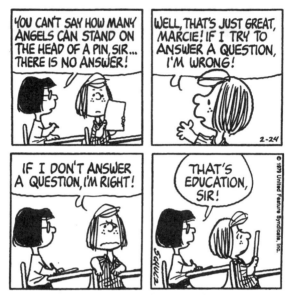

*Peanuts®* by Charles M. Schulz. Reprinted by permission of United Features Syndicate, Inc.

## Magical Thinking

Although many of Schulz's intuitive psychological insights are remarkable, some are virtually uncanny. The one that follows, for example, should have merited a Nobel Prize.

One of the most difficult emotional problems that confronts a psychiatrist is the obsessive-compulsive syndrome. This is a condition that causes much misery and even gross dysfunction. Classically, it consists of an obsessive thought coupled with a compulsive ritual, such as frequent hand washing to cleanse oneself of some impure feeling. Thankfully this condition is often effectively treated with medication. Still, the psychodynamics of the condition, as explained by Sigmund Freud, remain valid.

Freud postulated that the obsessive thought represents a wish, usually a forbidden wish, for which the subject feels guilty. He then goes through a symbolic ritual, whose function it is to neutralize or to undo the forbidden wish.

The reason one feels he must undo the wish is because unless it is undone, the wish will come true. In other words, the person believes he can make things happen by wishing them. We refer to this problem as "magical thinking," as if one's thoughts had magical powers.

Fortunately, our rational thinking usually prevails, and we realize that our thoughts do not make things happen. If wishes were that powerful, our thoughts would indeed be dangerous. How often do we think, under our breath, as it were, "Oh, drop dead" (Or "I wish I won the lottery" or "had a million bucks!") The fleeting hostile thoughts may occur whenever one is provoked, regardless of who it is that does the provocation, whether father, mother, husband, wife, son, daughter, or friend.

Countless patients have sought psychiatric treatment because of guilt feelings that occurred when someone died. We often find that the patient had at one time harbored a hostile wish, no matter how momentarily, toward that person, and therefore feels responsible for having caused his death.

Magical thinking probably begins at infancy. The infant feels hungry and wishes to be fed, and, lo and behold, his mother feeds him. He then concludes, "My desire for food controls my mother's actions. My wishes can control her behavior." This idea is expanded later in infancy in other situations, so that the infant comes to believe that he controls things and people with his thoughts.

This is a most frightening feeling. It is like being in possession of a nuclear weapon that is likely to go off whenever we wish. Imagine what it would be like if all your thoughts were immediately translated into action, and if every wish you had, regardless of its nature, would come true.

Schulz captures this concept in the following strip.

*Peanuts®* by Charles M. Schulz. Reprinted by permission of United Features Syndicate, Inc.

Linus, believing that his wish for the rain to go away indeed caused it to stop, is terrified by his awesome powers, and appeals to Lucy, for the safety and welfare of mankind, to hide him so that he cannot wreak destruction upon the entire world.

This is Schulz's psychological genius!

## Self-fulfilling Prophesies

There is an interesting phenomenon in human behavior, one which may result in unnecessary misery. Some people, if they suspect something bad may happen, may become so anxious about it, that the suspense is intolerable. To do away with the anxiety of the suspense, they go ahead and precipitate the very thing they fear, just to get it over with.

Let's suppose you anticipate something bad. O.K., there is a fifty percent chance of it happening, and the thought is distressing. But if you want to "get it over with," there is now a *one hundred percent* chance of it happening.

Charles Schulz has amazing insight into human behavior. Some people may feel that if they are going to suffer a loss, it is less distressing if they do it themselves than to be defeated by someone else, which is a blow to one's ego.

*Peanuts®* by Charles M. Schulz. Reprinted by permission of United Features Syndicate, Inc.

Linus knows that Lucy has a tendency to kick over his sand castle, and he hates to see all his effort go down the drain. That is certainly an unpleasant thought. Well, maybe she will, maybe she won't. But by beating her to it he *makes certain* that his hard work goes down the drain.

Suspense is part of life. Granted, it is uncomfortable, but don't let your ego increase the chances of your losing.

## The Insoluble Mystery

I have questioned Charles Schulz on his uncanny psychological insights and his ability to depict them graphically. Schulz just shrugged his shoulders, saying "I'm not as smart as you think."

This is an example of his innate psychological "smarts." Schulz asked me if I could shed some light on a theological issue that was bothering him. He then posed the age-old question: Why does a benevolent God permit so many terrible things to happen?

"You have already answered that question yourself," I said. Schulz looked bewildered. "I did?" he asked. "Where?"

"The answer, which appears in the Book of Job, is essentially that there is no logical answer. People who believe in God simply assume that He has valid reasons for allowing calamities to occur, but our limited human intelligence is incapable of grasping the divine wisdom," I said.

I then picked up a book of Schulz's cartoons and showed him the following strip.

*Peanuts*® by Charles M. Schulz. Reprinted by permission of United Features Syndicate, Inc.

## The Breakaways

There are two characters in "Peanuts" who may be seen as "breakaways" from society: Pig-Pen and Spike.

Pig-Pen is an extremely interesting character. He is a noncon-formist with his own values and standards, and seems to care lit-tle about what the world thinks of him.

In some ways, Pig-Pen may remind us of some of the non-conformists of the 1960s, who developed a counter-culture lifestyle, with disregard to and even antagonism toward prevailing values. While there is no denying that the world was in quite sad shape, there was little reason to believe that the lifestyle of flower children would result in a more stable and less hostile world. Yet the youth of the 1960s felt that anyone over thirty was not only obsolete but also had unhealthy values, and that only those enlightened by mind-expanding chemicals and liberated from traditional mores could save the world. And the 1960s was certainly not the only time in history when these kinds of factions developed.

*Peanuts®* by Charles M. Schulz. Reprinted by permission of United Features Syndicate, Inc.

Some of these nonconformists eventually came to suspect that they were not going to change the world, and that *they* might have to be the ones to adapt. However, those who left the mainstream to follow various gurus and realized that perhaps the Pied Piper was leading them to the river, found themselves essentially trapped. Marijuana, LSD, and other mind-altering drugs had become so much a part of their lives that they didn't know how to get along without them. Schulz has some profound insights into nonconformists.

*Peanuts®* by Charles M. Schulz. Reprinted by permission of United Features Syndicate, Inc.

If one is fortunate enough to realize that counter-culture behavior will impede one's adjustment to the realities of life, one can make changes early. Such insight may not occur in absence of a major crisis, but if it does occur, one should be grateful for coming to one's senses before it is too late.

*Peanuts*® by Charles M. Schulz. Reprinted by permission of United Features Syndicate, Inc.

Extending adolescent rebellion into the late teens or early twenties may be tolerable, but what happens when you really enter adulthood? How can one expect to survive, let alone succeed, if one persistently remains defiant of society's norms? A positive character trait is that which leads us to rethink certain traits as we mature.

Some may have tried to exit the counter-culture but gave up, considering it an act of futility. Even today, I encounter adolescents who realize that the use of drugs is destructive, yet feel they are unable to change, and the road to recovery is therefore often fraught with relapses.

*Peanuts*® by Charles M. Schulz. Reprinted by permission of United Features Syndicate, Inc.

While making a major change in one's lifestyle is not impossible, it does require a good deal of effort, what we may call a strong character. Many people are reluctant to invest the necessary effort, and some may resort to a fatalistic attitude: "I was born this way." This is a rationalization they use to justify their failure to make necessary changes. They may even succeed in convincing those around them that they are helpless.

*Peanuts®* by Charles M. Schulz. Reprinted by permission of United Features Syndicate, Inc.

No one gets dirty just by walking on the street, but Pig-Pen has succeeded in convincing Violet that this is just something that happens to him. He is therefore not responsible, nor is he able to change himself.

A frequently evoked rationalization is "peer pressure." Everyone in school smokes cigarettes, drinks, takes drugs, whatever. Not true. If you wish to associate with those who drink or drug, that is your decision. There is no denying that peer pressure exists, but everyone has the option to choose one's peer group.

*Peanuts*® by Charles M. Schulz. Reprinted by permission of United Features Syndicate, Inc.

Pig-Pen is dirty because of his "environment," but it is his choice to make mud puddles his environment.

Antisocial (what used to be called counter-culture) behavior can be very destructive. In the case of drugs, not only are some addictions extremely resistant to treatment but there is also the real possibility of persistent "flashbacks" and even brain damage. Even in absence of drug use, wasting the prime years of one's life, accumulating a record of anti-social acts that cannot be expunged, rather than getting an education can haunt a person throughout his life. There may indeed be a point of no return.

*Peanuts®* by Charles M. Schulz. Reprinted by permission of United Features Syndicate, Inc.

So much for Pig-Pen. The second breakaway is Spike, who is Snoopy's brother. Spike is essentially psychotic, and has broken with reality to live in the desert among cactuses. You will recall that Snoopy takes temporary leaves of absence from reality to live in fantasy, but always comes back to his reality of being a dog who is dependent for his food on a round-headed kid. Spike went just a bit further, having gone into a make-believe world and shut the door behind him.

For people around the psychotic, the person's break with reality can be very distressing. However, for the psychotic himself, living in fantasy land may be quite comfortable.

*Peanuts®* by Charles M. Schulz. Reprinted by permission of United Features Syndicate, Inc.

Some psychotics may consider themselves normal. Their family members may insist that they undergo treatment, but they deny any need. They may even claim psychiatric support for their position.

Reality can be difficult, and we may often have to make adjustments to its rigorous demands. Pretending is much easier, because all one need do is change the fantasy.

*Peanuts*® by Charles M. Schulz. Reprinted by permission of United Features Syndicate, Inc.

In reality, a school or other institution may decide on a particular dress code, and anyone wishing to remain affiliated must comply. In fantasy, no such compliance is necessary.

For some psychotics, the break with reality is due to their inability to socialize. Associating with people may be so frightening that they opt out. I witnessed this phenomenon when I worked in a state psychiatric hospital. It was tragic to observe the painful loneliness of these people. It is not that they did not crave companionship, but rather that they feared it. Yet associating with other psychotics in a state hospital did not provide the companionship they crave.

*Peanuts®* by Charles M. Schulz. Reprinted by permission of United Features Syndicate, Inc.

Some people with very profound feelings of inferiority believe that they cannot make it in reality, whereas in fantasy land there are no restrictions on what they may be. I have had patients who believed they were multibillionaires, top bank executives, and supreme court justices.

*Peanuts®* by Charles M. Schulz. Reprinted by permission of United Features Syndicate, Inc.

And, of course, one may be the athlete of the year.

*Peanuts®* by Charles M. Schulz. Reprinted by permission of United Features
Syndicate, Inc.

Patients would ask for weekend passes to spend time with
their families, and we were more than happy to have them do so.
It was not unusual, however, for patients to cut their visits short
and return to the safety of the hospital. Their contact with reality
had proved to be too challenging for them.

*Peanuts*® by Charles M. Schulz. Reprinted by permission of United Features Syndicate, Inc.

*Peanuts*® by Charles M. Schulz. Reprinted by permission of United Features Syndicate, Inc.

And so Spike leaves his family and reality for the safety of the desert. The last story he shares with Snoopy confirms our thesis of how difficult it is to be in reality.

*Peanuts*® by Charles M. Schulz. Reprinted by permission of United Features Syndicate, Inc.

Joining the other beagles on the fox hunt was a disaster. Whereas the other beagles participated in the hunt, Spike got lost, and actually had to depend on a fox to show him the way home. Snoopy, who represents the family, realizes that Spike must return to his make-believe world.

Someone may wish to point out that by reading "Peanuts" and imagining that dogs can think, write novels, and type, and that canaries can communicate with dogs, we too are living in a make-believe world. True, but as long as we can put the cartoon strips down and get back to our desks and jobs, we are okay.

## Say What You Mean

Sometimes we pick up a book on a subject that interests us, but after a few pages we are stymied because we don't understand it. We might say, "Wow, this is really profound stuff! This must be for advanced students, not for amateurs like me."

That's the way I used to feel, but my thinking has changed. I now believe that if a person has real clarity about his subject, he should make himself understood. I might not agree with Freud's psychological theories, but I understand what he is saying. However, some of Freud's disciples seem to be writing such "profound stuff" that I cannot grasp it. To me this says that their own grasp of the material was defective. Muddled writing usually indicates muddled thinking.

*Peanuts*® by Charles M. Schulz. Reprinted by permission of United Features Syndicate, Inc.

Many people share Peppermint Patty's opinion, that something that is easily understood cannot be good. The truth is just the opposite. A person with a good grasp of psychology can tell us what he means in a way that we can understand. This is why the

"Peanuts" cartoons communicate so well Schulz's psychological insights. He can tell us what he means.

## What Is Good Psychotherapy?

I have had ample opportunity to observe people undergoing psychotherapy. Some psychologists advocate long psychotherapy, while others advocate brief treatment. There are also various schools of psychotherapy, each championing a particular methodology.

The criteria of good psychotherapy is not its duration or technique, but rather what a person gets out of a session that they can apply to a real-life situation. Theories may be interesting, but unless the patient achieves a thorough understanding of why they are the way they are, treatment does not appreciably change their feeling or behavior.

*Peanuts®* by Charles M. Schulz. Reprinted by permission of United Features Syndicate, Inc.

When you have learned something from therapy that you can apply directly to life, then you've really learned something, and that is what makes good psychotherapy.

## A Spiritual Awakening

In the treatment of alcoholism, we refer to the moment of truth as a "spiritual awakening." After years and even decades of destructive drinking, during which time no amount of persuasion can convince the drinker that he has a problem, something occurs that brings him to his senses, and this is when recovery can begin.

Strangely enough, people who do not have an alcohol or similar problem may be at a disadvantage. They may go along with the routine of everyday life, behaving perfectly normally, not abusing their bodies yet also never giving much if any thought to just what they wish to accomplish with their lives. Unless some crisis occurs that shocks them out of their routine, they may never give a thought to the purpose of life. Yet as Socrates said, the unexamined life is not worth living.

It is our preoccupation with the demands of everyday existence that precludes our thinking about an ultimate goal. How fortunate we would be if we could come to this realization without experiencing a crisis.

*Peanuts®* by Charles M. Schulz. Reprinted by permission of United Features Syndicate, Inc.

Perhaps we can be as fortunate as Sally. If through routine we can realize that without an ultimate purpose in life much of what we do is futile, we can direct ourselves to look for a purpose in our existence.

## Endorsements

I have often wondered why people are impressed by celebrities' endorsements of products. I can understand an athlete promoting a piece of sport equipment or a health professional validating the claim of a particular medication (although sad to say, I still recall the commercial in which three out of four doctors smoked a certain brand of cigarettes!). But why on earth should I drink a certain soft drink because an outstanding athlete likes it?

It is difficult for me to accept that so many people are either so credulous or so stupid, yet the fact that millions are spent on endorsements by celebrities indicates this is so. I have the greatest respect for the mathematical genius of Einstein, but I am not impressed by his religious ideas; his excellence in one field does not make him an authority in another. Nor would Arturo Toscanini's musical genius make him an authority on anything but music.

*Peanuts*® by Charles M. Schulz. Reprinted by permission of United Features Syndicate, Inc.

*Peanuts®* by Charles M. Schulz. Reprinted by permission of United Features Syndicate, Inc.

## Once Upon a Time

This strip impressed me for nostalgic reasons.

Perhaps I long for the days when authority was authority, when parents, teachers, principals, and courts were obeyed. Whatever drawbacks that system had, it was far better than the anarchy of today, which, between sexual promiscuity, uncontrolled intoxication with chemicals, and rampant crime threatens our existence as a species.

When I was a student in Lloyd Street Elementary school, our principal was Miss Ehbets. Coming from a religious home, I had a concept of God as being all-powerful. In fact, God was almost as powerful as Miss Ehbets. To be told "Report to the principal's office" was far worse than being told that you would be drawn and quartered. The principal was viewed with both reverence and dread.

As a medical student, I did routine physical examinations in a hospital for the chronically mentally disabled. Imagine the shock when on the list of patients I was to examine was Pauline Ehbets! My Miss Ehbets? In a hospital for the chronically insane? My worst fears were confirmed when the nurse wheeled in a little frail, aged lady, who had deteriorated with senility. It is now forty years later, and I still recall the shock of that moment. My mentor, a woman I admired and feared, now stricken with mental illness. It was more than I could absorb.

Once upon a time there was respect for authority. Perhaps it is wishful thinking, that such reverence may yet recur.

## It Is Someone Else's Fault

As we've seen, Peppermint Patty refuses to assume responsibility for getting poor grades, and tries to place the blame on everyone else. But this is hardly unique to Patty. Society, as a whole, is into the blaming game.

Crime is committed by people who are "deprived of opportunity to earn an honest living. It's society's fault." Young people become addicted to drugs because the "schools are not doing an adequate job." Again, it's society's fault.

Hogwash. A comparison of two communities of equal population, one economically deprived and the other affluent, will show an equal incidence of crime and drugs in each.

People's behaviors are their own doings. Things will not change so long as we hide behind the apron strings of "society."

*Peanuts*® by Charles M. Schulz. Reprinted by permission of United Features Syndicate, Inc.

## Philanthropy at Its Worst

It is wonderful to help others, and we should all be doing more of it. Ideally, however, we should be doing it of our own free will, and with our own funds.

The government has assumed the role of caring for the needy, and while this is certainly a laudable cause, the undeniable fact is that in many social welfare programs, only a fraction of the money allotted actually gets to those in need. Much of the money ends up in one or another aspect of an immense bureaucracy.

Every once in a while a whistle is blown on these abuses, but they continue nevertheless. I seriously doubt that these abuses would exist if those dispensing the funds were spending their own money. There would certainly be a much greater accountability and much less waste.

*Peanuts*® by Charles M. Schulz. Reprinted by permission of United Features Syndicate, Inc.

## Put Your Money Where Your Mouth Is

There are many advocacy groups for a variety of causes, and, of course, one may agree or disagree with any of them. We must show tolerance for all opinions, but it is a bit annoying when one sees gross inconsistencies within a cause or belief system.

For example, there are some people who champion animals' rights, and oppose the slaughtering of animals for human consumption. Some of them, however, are not averse to wearing comfortable leather shoes, which are rather unlikely to have been manufactured from hides of animals who died a natural death.

*Peanuts®* by Charles M. Schulz. Reprinted by permission of United Features Syndicate, Inc.

If you are going to fight for a cause, then be sincere.

## Lastly, for Charlie, Marcie, Schroeder, Patty, and the whole gang

As I discussed, Marcie differs from Schoeder in that her single-mindedness does not preclude her being in love. It is of interest, however, that just as Marcie has developed a paternalistic relationship toward Peppermint Patty, this attitude affects her love life as well. Marcie feels sorry for Charlie Brown, and shows it in a very human way.

*Peanuts®* by Charles M. Schulz. Reprinted by permission of United Features
Syndicate, Inc.

Marcie likes and is mad at Charlie at the same time. She feels
threatened for having succumbed to emotion, and feels she must
somehow explain it away. Just how absurd rationalizations can
get is indicated by Marcie's attributing her affection for Charlie
Brown to her being angry at him! The Peanuts gang are just like
us! Thank you Charles Schulz for so lovingly illustrating our
foibles.